CAT

P9-DBR-150

Design Companion
for the Digital Artist

FLORIDA TECHNICAL COLLEGE LIBRARY
12689 CHALLENGER PARKWAY
SUITE 130
ORLANDO, FL 32826

Florida Technical College Library
12900 Challenger Prkwy.
Orlando, FL 32826

Florida Technical College Library
12900 Challenger Prkwy.
Orlando, FL 32826

Design Companion
for the Digital Artist

AGAINST THE CLOCK

PERFORMANCE SUPPORT & TRAINING SYSTEMS

Upper Saddle River, NJ 07458

Library of Congress Cataloging-in-Publication Data

Design companion for the digital artist
    p. cm. — (Against the Clock series)
    ISBN 0-13-091237-9
    1. Graphic Arts—Technique. 2. Commercial Art—Technique. I. Series

NC845 .D47 2002
741.6--dc21   2001034594

Editor-in-Chief: Stephen Helba
Director of Production and Manufacturing: Bruce Johnson
Executive Editor: Elizabeth Sugg
Managing Editor-Editorial: Judy Casillo
Editorial Assistant: Anita Rhodes
Managing Editor-Production: Mary Carnis
Production Editor: Denise Brown
Composition: Against the Clock, Inc.
Design Director: Cheryl Asherman
Senior Design Coordinator: Miguel Ortiz
Cover Design: LaFortezza Design Group, Inc.
Interior Design: Lee Goldstein
Printer/Binder: RR Donnelley & Sons

Pearson Education LTD.
Pearson Education Australia PTY, Limited
Pearson Education Singapore, Pte. Ltd
Pearson Education North Asia Ltd
Pearson Education Canada, Ltd.
Pearson Educación de Mexico, S.A. de C.V.
Pearson Education -- Japan
Pearson Education Malaysia, Pte. Ltd
Pearson Education, Upper Saddle River, New Jersey

A portion of the images supplied in this book are Copyright © PhotoDisc, Inc., 201 Fourth Ave., Seattle, WA 98121. These images are the sole property of PhotoDisc and are used by Against The Clock with the permission of the owners.

Against The Clock and the Against The Clock logo are trademarks of Against The Clock, Inc., registered in the United States and elsewhere. References to and instructional materials provided for any particular application program, operating system, hardware platform, or other commercially available product or products do not represent an endorsement of such product or products by Against The Clock, Inc. or Prentice Hall, Inc.

Photoshop, Acrobat, Adobe Type Manager, Illustrator, InDesign, PageMaker, Premiere, and PostScript are trademarks of Adobe Systems Incorporated. Macintosh is a trademark of Apple Computer, Inc. Macromedia Flash, FreeHand, Dreamweaver, FireWorks and Director are registered trademarks of Macromedia, Inc. CorelDRAW! and Painter are trademarks of Corel Corporation. FrontPage, Publisher, PowerPoint, Word, Excel, Office, Microsoft, MS-DOS, Windows, and Windows NT are either registered trademarks or trademarks of Microsoft Corporation. QuarkXPress is a registered trademark of Quark, Inc.

™ and © 2000 Burger King Brands, Inc.

Other products and company names mentioned herein may be the trademarks of their respective owners.

Copyright © 2002 by Pearson Education, Inc. Upper Saddle River, New Jersey 07458. All rights reserved. Printed in the United States of America. This publication is protected by Copyright and permission should be obtained from the publisher prior to any prohibited reproduction, storage in a retrieval system, or transmission in any form or by any means, electronic, mechanical, photocopying, recording, or likewise. For information regarding permission(s), write to: Rights and Permissions Department.

10 9 8 7 6 5 4 3 2

ISBN 0-13-091237-9

Contents

Introduction   1
    From a Designer's Point of View   1
    Quick Checklist for Designers   2

Section 1 Getting the Idea   3

    CHAPTER 1 A HARD LOOK AT CREATIVITY   7
    The Five Forces of Creativity   7
    Becoming Creative   8
        Creativity Is Not a Talent   9
    Tips for Fueling Creatively   9
        Stand on Your Head   9
        The Inspiration File   9
        Change Your Perspective   10
        Know Your Market   10

    CHAPTER 2 DEVELOPING THE CONCEPT   13
    Brainstorming with Words   14
    Visual Brainstorming   16
    Dealing with Creative Block   18
        Rationalization   18
        Procrastination   18
        Burn Out   19
        Overwork   19
        "I'm not a creative person."   19

CHAPTER 3 ABSTRACTION, SYMBOLISM, AND VISUAL METAPHOR 21

Abstraction 21
Symbolism and the Visual Metaphor 22
　　How are Symbols Used? 22
　　Modern Symbolism 23
Propaganda and Motivational Psychology 24
　　Visual Overload 25
　　Icons 25
Dealing with the Cliché 26
Color Symbolism 26
　　White 26
　　Yellow 27
　　Green 27
　　Red 28
　　Purple 28
　　Pink 28
　　Blue 28
　　Black 29
　　Grey 29
Summing it All Up 29

CHAPTER 4 PUTTING IT ALL TOGETHER 31

The Production Process 31
　　Thumbnails 32
　　Roughs 33
　　Proof 34
Chart Your Process 35

SECTION 1 PROJECTS 37

A New Face on Sunny Island 38
Reinventing the Zoo 39
So Long, Crazy Harry 40

Section 2 Using the Elements 41

CHAPTER 5 SHAPE/CONTAINER RELATIONSHIP 43

Looking at the Container 43
　　Placing a Shape Within the Container 44
　　Real-World Shape/Container Relationships 45
Balance — Use of Space 45
　　The Theory from a Designer's Viewpoint 45

Types of Balance 46
    Formal (Symmetrical) Balance 46
    Informal (Asymmetrical) Balance 47
    Radial Balance 48
Negative and Positive Space 49
    The Theory From a Designer's Viewpoint 49

CHAPTER 6 LAYOUT 53

Use Master Pages to Design More Effectively 54
Layout Development 54
Creating Visual Interest 56
    Columns 56
    The "Z" 57
    The Focal Point of the Page 58
    Rhythm 58
    Unity 58
Layout Makeovers 59

CHAPTER 7 LINE 61

Lines From a Designer's Viewpoint 61
    Lines as Objects: Physical Characteristics of Lines 61
    Line Direction, Implication, and Emotion 62
The Emotional Content of a Line 64

CHAPTER 8 TYPE 65

Type Categories 65
    Serif Type 65
    Sans-Serif Type 66
    Script (Invitation) Type 66
    Decorative Type 66
    Pi (Symbol) Type 66
Type Families 67
Kerning, Tracking, and Leading 68
Type Do's and Don'ts 69
    DO: 69
    DON'T: 71
Using Type to Create a Mood or Idea 71

CHAPTER 9 COLOR   77

Color Perception and Meaning   77
   Memory Color   77
   Complementary Colors   79
Using the Proper Color Mode   79
   Printing Processes   77
   Spot Color   80
   RGB Color   82
   Color Management   82
   Color Viewing   83
   Black-and-White (or Green-and-White...)   83
Suggestions for Using Color   84

CHAPTER 10 PAPER, BINDING, AND FINISHING   85

The Best Place to Start is at the End   85
   A Few Words about Imposition   87
   Size Does Matter, Especially to the Postal Service 88
Paper Type, Color, and Texture   88
The Right Paper for the Job   90
Finishing Choices   91
   Folding   91
   Diecutting   92
   Embossing, Foil Stamping, and Lamination   92
   Varnish   92
In Conclusion   92

CHAPTER 11 USING PICTURES EFFECTIVELY   93

Picture Clarity   93
Composition   94
Framing the Subject   95
Move Closer   95
Pictures of People   96
   Line of Sight   96
   Layouts for People Pictures   97
Enhance Visual Impact   98
   The Photograph as an Object   98
   The Photograph as a Floating Object   98
   Other Effects   99

SECTION 2 PROJECTS   101

A New Face on Sunny Island   102
Reinventing the Zoo   103
So Long, Crazy Harry   104

Section 3 The Graphic Design Marketplace 105

CHAPTER 12 PUBLICATION DESIGN 111

Specialties within Publication Design 111
Special Markets — Catalog Design 113
Hints for Successful Publication Design 114
Breaking into the Market 115
Start Small, Start Local 115

CHAPTER 13 ILLUSTRATION 117

Information Graphics 117
Early Information Graphics 118
The Importance of Information Graphics 118
Ethical Considerations 119
Technical Illustration 119
Editorial Illustration 120
Defining Your Style 120
Editorial Illustration Specialties 120
Breaking into the Market 125

CHAPTER 14 CORPORATE IDENTITY 127

Hallmarks of Good Logos 128
The Client Is Always Right? 128
"I don't know what I want. I'll know it when I see it." 128
"This is exactly what I want..." 130

CHAPTER 15 POINT-OF-PURCHASE DISPLAY AND PACKAGING 133

Point-of-Purchase Display 133
Types of POP 135
Packaging 136
Special Design Concerns for Packaging 137
Special Market Segment — Music Industry Design 137

CHAPTER 16 ADVERTISING DESIGN 139

So What's It All About, Anyway? 140
Know Your Market 141
Promise, Amplify, Proof, Action 142
Developing a Full Campaign 143
Special Market Opportunity — Writing Copy 143
Breaking into the Market 144

CHAPTER 17 WEB DESIGN AND MULTIMEDIA   145

Designing for the Web   145
What You See May Not Be What You Get   148
     Fonts   149
     Colors   149
     Monitor size   150
     File Size and Download Time   150
Multimedia Design   151
     Presentations   151
     Interactive CD-ROMs   152
     Interactive Kiosks   153

Gallery   **155**

Glossary

Index

Preface

The *Against The Clock Companion Series* offers insight into fundamental artistic issues. It covers the details of broad design topics such as:

The basic rules of good design,

The proper and effective use of color,

The history and application of typography,

Typography's role in the design process,

The principles underlying proven and compelling Web site design.

The *Against The Clock Companion Series* works together with application-specific libraries of training and skills-development books. The books in the series provide background in fundamental design and artistic issues. They complement the hands-on, skills-based approach of the *Against the Clock* and other applications titles. The series:

Contains **richly illustrated real-world examples** of commercial and institutional artwork, designs, packaging, and other creative assignments;

Provides the reasoning behind the **creative strategies, production methodologies, and distribution models** — in the words of the artists who provided them;

Addresses the four most important disciplines critical to successful use of computer arts applications: **design, color, typography, and Web page design**;

Presents the material in a **friendly and easy-to-understand** manner, rather than relying on technical jargon or obsolete terminology.

The books in the Companion Series are:

Design Companion for the Digital Artist (ISBN: 0-13-091237-9)

Typography Companion for the Digital Artist (ISBN: 0-13-040993-6)

Web Design Companion for the Digital Artist (ISBN: 0-13-097355-6)

Color Companion for the Digital Artist (ISBN: 0-13-097524-9)

We hope that you'll find the books as effective and useful as we found them exciting and fun to develop. As always, we welcome any comments you might have that will make the next editions of the books even better. Please feel free to contact us at computer_arts@prenhall.com.

About Against The Clock

Against The Clock (ATC) was founded in 1990 and went on to become one of the nation's leading systems integration and training firms. The organization, founded by Ellenn Behoriam, specialized in developing custom training materials for clients such as L.L. Bean, *The New England Journal of Medicine*, the Smithsonian, the National Education Association, *Air & Space Magazine*, Publishers Clearing House, the National Wildlife Society, Home Shopping Network, and many others.

Building on their lengthy experience creating focused and structured training materials, ATC's management team began working with major publishers in the mid-nineties to produce high-quality application and workflow-specific training aids. In 1996, ATC introduced the highly popular "Creative Techniques" series, which focused on real-world examples of award-winning commercial design, imaging, and Web page development. Working with Adobe Press, they also developed successful management books, including *Workflow Reengineering*, which won the IDIA award as most effective book of the year in 1997.

In 1998, the company entered into a long-term relationship with Prentice Hall/Pearson Education. This relationship allows ATC to focus on bringing high-quality content to the marketplace to address up-to-the-minute software releases. The Against The Clock library has grown to include over 35 titles — focusing on all aspects of computer arts. From illustration to Web site design, from image to animation, and from page layout to effective production techniques, the series is highly-regarded and is recognized as one of the most powerful teaching and training tools in the industry.

Against The Clock, Inc. is located in Tampa, Florida and can be found on the Web at www.againsttheclock.com.

About the Authors

Valan Evers lives and plays in South Florida. She has been on the faculty of the Art Institute of Fort Lauderdale for the past 12 years. Her digital illustrations have appeared on magazine covers and were featured in the book, *CYBERDESIGN: Computer Manipulated Photography* by Rockport Publishers. Her work was chosen to be included in the 1999 release of the book, *Digital Photo 1*, by the prestigious publisher of fine art books, Graphis. Most of her work hangs in galleries, private, and corporate collections. She also has a limited edition of posters and postcards. Her abiding passions (besides making art) are diving, underwater photography, and mythology. She earned her Masters Degree in Computer Illustration/Underwater Photography, and did her thesis on digital narratives of oceanic mythology.

Erika Kendra lives in Los Angeles, where she operates under the guise of The Right Brain. She has been editing and designing books for the printing and graphic design communities for five years; she also provides desktop publishing and digital prepress consulting and training for the printing industry. When she isn't being manipulated by her cats, she can usually be found reading archaic literature, attending Renaissance festivals, or enjoying the Southern California sun. She earned a BA in History and a BA in English Literature from the University of Pittsburgh.

Acknowledgements

I would like to thank the writers, editors, illustrators and production staff who have worked long and hard to complete the Against The Clock series.

Thank you to our technical team of teaching professionals whose comments and expertise contributed to the success of this book, including Doris Anton of the Wichita Area Technical College, Dee A. Colvin, of the Univeristy of North Florida, Suzanne Lambert of Broward Community College, and Barry Erdeljon of Marymount University.

A big thank you to all of the artists who contributed their work in the gallery and throughout this book.

Thank you to Judy Casillo, Developmental Editor, and Denise Brown, Production Editor, for their guidance, patience, and attention to detail.

INTRODUCTION

From a Designer's Point of View

When we, as graphic designers, illustrators, or artists think of design, we frequently think in terms of the elements of design — line, shape, negative and positive space, rhythm, continuity, balance, and all the other items we use to compose some project.

Design is much more than that, more than the sum of those parts. Think of all the things that are designed. In a matter of a few moments it is possible to list hundreds of things: airplanes, buildings, books, clothing, shaving cans, gardening tools, furniture. The list is seemingly endless. So what is "design"?

In *An Approach to Design*, Norman Newton (designer and author) wrote, "In every problem of design, the most fundamental issue is some human need, some maladjustment or inadequacy between people and their environment that awaits correction."

This book guides you through the elements of graphic design, from idea conception to final piece. Section 1 focuses on creativity — how you can develop a successful solution for any design problem. We will offer suggestions for fueling your creative juices, and provide insight into the things you should know before ever picking up a pencil. Three projects at the end of the section allow you to put these ideas to work. We've modeled the projects after real-world design problems, to give you an idea of what you might encounter in your career as a graphic designer.

Section 2 focuses on the physical elements of design: shape/container relationship, layout, line, type, color, paper and finishing choices, and pictures. We examine each of these elements in detail, offering numerous conceptual and real-world examples throughout the section. Section 2 concludes with three projects that will test your ability to use what you learn about the elements of design. Again, the projects are structured to reflect what you will find in the real world of graphic design.

Section 3 breaks down the graphic design market. Graphic designers do not operate in a vacuum; many people are involved in producing the final piece. We will provide a brief description of these different roles. We also examine the different specialties within graphic design, providing examples and offering suggestions for breaking into the different markets. Finally, a Gallery of Graphic Design provides full color examples of the concepts we've discussed throughout the book.

Quick Checklist for Designers

We present here a list of commandments for all designers. They will make your work, and your life, a lot easier. We'll discuss them at greater length throughout this book.

- Be certain you completely understand the design problem.

- Know your target market (trends, styles, and visual preferences.)

- Listen to the client for valuable data.

- Brainstorm everything you know about the client, the audience, and the competition.

- Know what materials are available to you (print media, electronic media, photos, type, layout software, clip art, etc.)

- Know the most appropriate media for the project (pen and ink, halftone 2-color print, 4-color, magazine, newspaper, billboard, multimedia, etc.)

- Know the client's design specifications (if any exist.)

- Know your budget.

- Know the deadlines. Pace mini-deadlines accordingly.

Two additional tips to keep in mind. The best design is the one which is the best visual solution, is aimed squarely at the target market, is aesthetically pleasing, is within the budget, and meets the deadline.

Lastly, and very importantly — do not fall in love with your idea. Commercial art is not personal art. You may think your design is the best thing in the world, the most beautiful picture ever created by any human. You spent hours to make it work. But your client hates it, the art director makes some changes, or it just doesn't solve the problem well. This only creates hostility between the people involved, which doesn't make a very good working relationship. Keep your beautiful concept, put it in a frame on your wall, but remember that your client's opinion does matter since they are paying for the project.

GETTING THE IDEA

*I believe in Michaelangelo, Velasquez, and Rembrandt;
in the might of design, the mystery of color, the redemption
of all things by Beauty everlasting, and the message of Art
that has made these hands blessed.*

—GEORGE BERNARD SHAW

3

Graphic design is the process of solving a problem visually. How can you communicate the intended message with one (or a few) image, delivered in a limited space, without lengthy contextual explanation? The goal of graphic design is not to come up with the prettiest, funniest, or most colorful picture. Rather, the goal graphic design is to create a visual solution to a communication problem.

When a graphic designer is hired, it is usually to design a specific piece of commercial artwork. A brochure is needed, or a company needs a logo, or an advertisement is needed to promote a product — all of these projects have obvious purposes. A graphic designer does more than simply decorate. Design is decidedly goal-driven; it is always a purposeful endeavor, with a clear outcome fixed in the front of the designer's mind.

People generally assume that brilliant graphic design is a matter of being able to draw better than the average person. Graphic design, however, is not necessarily the result of artistic talent. The most overlooked factor in graphic design is the ability to come up with a good, solid idea. All the fancy software in the world cannot save a poorly conceived idea. Design and composition skills can be taught. But can concept development be taught?

The answer is yes, graphic design most definitely can be taught. Not in the same way that mechanical skills are taught; there is no formula that guarantees a brilliant design solution every time. There is, however, a method — a systematic approach to the design process, which, if used consistently, produces solid answers to design problems.

A designer does not arrive at a visual solution through happenstance. Many people, when given a design job, rush right to the final step — producing the piece. In their haste to produce a tangible finished ad, brochure, or report, they gallop right into production with scarcely a thought to the work of concept development. They have a hazy idea of what the piece is going to say, they have a vague idea of the layout, the type treatment, and the visual elements, but they assume that the issues will work themselves out as they are encountered in the production process.

It seems obvious to include your client in the process, but designers have a bad tendency to spring their plans, full-blown, on clients. Clients are always more receptive to innovative solutions if they feel they have had some input. This *does not* mean to allow your clients to design — designing is your job. You will, at some point in your career, encounter a client who thinks they know exactly what they want, you only need to draw it. This is the *worst* situation you can be in, since the client's ideas aren't always the most effective communication solutions. It's your job to convince clients to let you do your job. Encourage your clients' input, ask them what they think the problem is, who their competition is, what look or style they might want, and if they have any data or information that will help you to create an effective design.

The design process should always begin with a clear idea of the problem that needs solving. This seems obvious, but it is a huge stumbling block in the creation of a successful design.

The next logical step in the design process should be to choose the best media for the job. Again, this seems obvious, but it is ironic how many times a designer has been hired to create a brochure, when a magazine or newspaper ad was the proper vehicle for the visual solution.

Do not wait for creativity. A professional creates best to deadlines because deadlines force the use of tested methods for generating ideas. Over time, we each work out our own personal style. The Concept section of this book has some great suggestions for beginning the process. After brainstorming ideas, test ideas for practicality, usability, budget constraints, and production difficulties. Check in with your client after this step for encouragement, feedback, and participation.

Successful design is much more than something that looks nice. Success is judged by a much more concrete criteria than that which we use to evaluate personal art. A successful designer is more than a skilled artist. We are, first and foremost, informed visual problem solvers. Evaluate your design ideas based on the following criteria:

- Does the idea answer a specific problem or goal?

- Is the idea creative and original?

- Is the idea an appropriate treatment for the intended media?

- Will the idea work within the budget?

- Is the idea appropriate for both the client and the target audience?

- Is the idea appropriate for the intended message?

- Is your client happy with the idea?

If you have a poorly visualized, poorly planned design, the results can range from merely ineffective to catastrophic. Graphic design is largely a matter of discipline, rather than wildly unbridled talent. The first section of this book is dedicated to supporting this point by providing a variety of time-tested methods for idea generation. It deals with the misconceptions about achieving creative results, and suggests ways that you can train yourself to think creatively.

CHAPTER 1

A Hard Look at Creativity

A long-delayed question is, how does it happen that very young children, all of whom quite naturally absorb great quantities of visual information, grow up to be visually illiterate? The answer, as far as I can make out, is that this early capability is simply beaten out of them by the educational process.

—GEORGE NELSON, *HOW TO SEE*, LITTLE, BROWN: BOSTON, 1977

Walter Gropius (leader of the Bauhaus) in a treatise on the role of an artist in the age of the Industrial Revolution, stated: "…for the artist possesses the ability to breathe soul into the lifeless product of the machine, and his creative powers continue to live within it as a long ferment. His collaboration is not a luxury, not a pleasing adjunct; it must become an indispensable component of the total output of modern industry."

The Five Forces of Creativity

Five forces enable creativity:

Inspiration, motivation, frustration, intuition, and curiosity

How do you get a great idea? Does it come to you fully developed? Does it just sort of smack you between the eyes, in bright glowing colors? You're lucky if this happens to you more than a few times in your life. For most of us, the creative process starts not by a lucky quirk of inspiration, but with one of the four other major forces which help to stimulate ideas.

Motivation is a drive to attain a goal, reach a solution, or find an answer. Design, in general, is goal-driven, since we are usually trying to meet a deadline. Motivation is a compelling force, and can be a powerful tool for a self-disciplined person. This person has a great stubbornness and a willingness to plough through the design process to reach a goal.

Frustration (however unlikely this may seem) can be a great help in creative problem-solving. Frustration creates great energy, which can be refocused into a driving force. Frustration can also help to force reorganization, dividing design problems into more workable chunks. Many creative people do their best work when frustrated.

Have you ever had a hunch? You "just knew" the answer. This is the subconscious at work. People who get hunches are tapping into that huge library of stored data in their heads. Intuition is not a predictable source of creativity, but the results can be brilliant.

The final force behind creativity is curiosity. People sometimes prefer to stay comfortably in a state of ignorance; resist this kind of complacency. Get in the habit of asking questions. Try to ask unusual questions, inappropriate questions, silly questions. Think outside of the box, and welcome answers from outside the box.

Becoming Creative

Webster defines *creative* as "resulting from originality of thought or expression." Following this definition, everyone is by nature a creative person. We all have the ability to come up with an original thought or expression. As children we are encouraged to let our imaginations run wild. Somewhere along the way, we are expected to Grow Up. The key to being truly creative is to get out of your own way. "Thinking outside of the box"—thinking about things differently than the average person would is a designer's mantra.

Following are some suggestions for keeping your inner child alive:

- Be curious

- Be open-minded

- Be strongly purposeful

- Be ready at all times to be inspired

- Think improbable thoughts

- Don't be serious all the time

- Make puns

- Juxtapose ideas and imagery

- Use metaphors

- Discard no idea, no matter how absurd

- Generate many answers — the more, the better!

- Know that inspiration is a controllable element

CREATIVITY IS NOT A TALENT

Look at the above list. Notice that the word "talent" is not mentioned once. Being creative does not require a particular talent. Talent is a gift, more closely aligned with potential; talent is a matter of nature.

Creativity, however, is a product of nurture. To be a creative person, treat yourself as a creative person. It is not enough to simply *think* of yourself as creative; rather, do the things that creative people do. Act as if you are a creative person; allow yourself to respond in the way you would allow a creative person to respond. Once you get into the habit of acting creatively, you'll notice that eventually this kind of response doesn't have to be forced.

One of the joys of being a creative person is that other people come to expect the unexpected. Be flamboyant, be outrageous, be unusual, be irreverent, be anything you want to be. There are very few rules to creativity. The only one is to never settle for something less than creativity.

Tips for Fueling Creatively

STAND ON YOUR HEAD

Or hula-hoop, or play hopscotch, or ride a dirt bike. Most designers have some kind of instrument that sparks the creative fires. Whether it is yoga, baking, singing at the top of your lungs, dancing with your cat, or listening to a particular kind of music, experiment to find what helps you work. You might find that your best work comes from standing on your head in the corner. Do it! No matter how strange it may seem to other people, harness whatever you like to be creative.

THE INSPIRATION FILE

Practically every designer (graphic designer, clothes designer, architect, chef, or hair stylist) shares a common denominator — they all have a folder, file drawer, cabinet, or scrapbook of inspiring things. Whether it's called a sourcebook, idea book, inspiration file, or something else, designers are avid collectors of things that inspire their creativity.

Simply having an inspiration file will help fuel your creativity since you are paying more attention to what you see. While you are looking for things to collect, you're opening yourself to a wider range of visual cues by paying attention to what you may have overlooked in the course of everyday life. You can also use your inspiration file to jump-start your imagination if you hit a creative block.

One designer shared her inspiration file with us — it's a suitcase-sized portfolio box with acetate pages like a scrapbook, and room for loose items. Her inspiration file is filled with items that she picked up and thought were worth saving: feathers, seashells, bits of ribbon, pictures that "lured" her, comic books, postcards from Istanbul and Norway, a letter written in Japanese, ads she admired, matchbooks, and a cancelled postage stamp from the Arctic Circle.

Your inspiration file can contain anything—bits of fabric, illustrations, postcards, work you admire in your field, unusual visual solutions, visual jokes, scraps of paper with written notes, fragments of ideas you've had, rough sketches of designs, doodles. Anything that you might look at for more than a minute is usually a good candidate for your collection. Something is worth saving if:

- It amuses you

- It amazes you

- You think it is pretty, beautiful, serene, soothing, etc.

- You find it disturbing, gross, haunting, scary, depressing, etc.

- The texture is intriguing

- You love the colors

- You wonder how it was made

- You know what is wrong with it, and how to make the design better

CHANGE YOUR PERSPECTIVE

Have you ever stared at your face in the mirror for so long that it no longer makes sense? When you are designing something, you probably sit in the same chair at the same desk in the same room every day. You will have the same sensory cues around you, the same pictures on the wall, the same air conditioner droning in the background... get the point?

Try moving to another place. Fresh design concepts may require fresh surroundings. Take your sketchbook outside, up to the roof, to a cafe, or to a subway or train station. Go somewhere you normally don't go to, and look at the world around you. Leave your preconceived ideas in your same old chair, and just watch. This will help you to develop a heightened awareness of the world around you, which will give your creativity a boost.

KNOW YOUR MARKET

One of the most important facets of design is to know who you are designing for. This does not mean the client, but the ultimate target for your design — or your *target market*. Demographics play a key role in determining what kind of design to use. A design that communicates well with a 16 to 25-year-old audience living in New York City will not be as effective if you are trying to communicate with 40 to 50-year-old house-wives living in Alabama. Age, gender, nationality, economic status, and geographic region can all dictate some aspects of your design.

You are probably familiar with the concept of target audience, even if you don't realize it. Consider television. Certain shows appeal to different age groups; some shows are specifically designed to attract female viewers, while others are intended for men. Make a list of three or four shows that you watch, then list a few reasons why you like to watch them. This is a great way to determine what your own demographic group might find appealing. Of course this doesn't mean that every person who matches your demographic statistics will like the same things, but it is a good starting point.

To further illustrate the concept of target marketing, walk through any mall or shopping plaza. Which stores would you go in? Which stores do you never go to? Pick one of the stores you never go to, and sit outside of it for an hour, taking note of the people who do shop there. Do you notice anything that those people have in common? Are they primarily women or men? Do they seem to be the same age group? Nationality or race? Once you've got an idea of the shoppers' characteristics, go into the store and look around. What colors are predominant in the store's design? What kind and color of lighting is used? What do the fixtures look like? Are there any predominant shapes?

Research groups spend countless hours and dollars studying what appeals to different kinds of people... what colors, attitudes, layouts, and approaches most effectively communicate to certain demographic groups. If you have the opportunity, read a book or take a class on basic market-ing concepts. Even if this isn't an option, there are a few basic questions that you can ask to help you on the path to an effective design solution. Look at your problem and try to determine who the client is trying to communicate with. Then ask:

- What are these people's interests?
- What motivates them?
- What would appeal to them?
- Who are their role models?

When you approach a design problem, try to put yourself into your audience's shoes. Most people are able to briefly think from another's perspective; the trick is to be that person a bit longer.

CHAPTER 2

Developing the Concept

Imagination… in truth, is but another name for power and clearest insight.

—WILLIAM WORDSWORTH

Perhaps the most vital and overlooked aspect of graphic design the development of a strong concept. How do you come up with a design idea? Does it simply come to you, fully developed? Does it smack you on the forehead in bright glowing colors? Did a muse visit you in a dream? For most of us, the creative process does not begin with some lucky quirk of inspiration, but from an ordered and disciplined process.

As a graphic designer it is your job to develop ideas, to present the best solution for your client's communication problem. Once you understand the problem (i.e., what the client needs, whether it is a logo, newsletter, or advertisement), you must develop an idea. So rather than wait for the design fairies to visit while you sleep, consider other methods of developing an idea.

The first step of the graphic design process is brainstorming. When you begin any brainstorm activity, keep two important factors in mind. Remember that brainstorming is itself a process; you have to give the process a chance to work. Even if you can't think of anything in the first few minutes, keep at it. If the ideas were that easy to come by, we wouldn't have to brainstorm. Regardless of which brainstorm technique you use, don't stop too soon in the process.

The second factor to remember is that there are no bad ideas. Brainstorming does not intend to reveal "right" or "wrong" answers; at this stage you are only looking for *an* answer. Brainstorming attempts to give you a jumping point, not an immediate solution. Keep all your ideas in mind, no matter how silly, convoluted, or disconnected an idea may initially seem.

Begin any brainstorm activity by writing down the problem. The first solutions that come to mind are likely to be cliche, since our minds almost always have preconceived ideas based on things we've already seen. Go ahead and write down the cliches, since you may find them useful later as a starting point for something new. Once you get that out of the way, move on to more creative solutions.

Brainstorming with Words

When you're looking for ideas, remember that words can be very powerful. Depending on your particular problem, word play can be a powerful tool. Go back to your original ideas, the cliched ones. Look for synonyms, antonyms, rhyming words, or analogies that may lead to new solutions for old problems.

If you were asked to design a concept for a new space-aged kids' cereal, you probably wouldn't call it "Space-Aged Kids' Cereal." Instead, think of the words that might suggest "space-aged" without being so literal. Orbit, moon, star, and galaxy are all good alternatives to "outerspace." "Cereal" might be (and is, if you've looked in a grocery store lately) flakes, Os, or crunch.

Consider the colors used in a women's clothing catalog. Clothing is usually described as "periwinkle" instead of blue or "sun" instead of yellow. Cars are painted "steel" or "granite" instead of grey. Even without a picture, your choice of words to describe something can create a specific visual image.

Analogies are also useful to fuel your creative juices to a new solution. Consider the emotion or message you are trying to convey in your design, and make a list of analogies. If your assignment is to advertise a new line of shampoo, what would using that shampoo be like? Consider the Irish Spring ads in the mid 1980s — isolated mountain waterfalls and clear streams flowing through lush green countrysides. This implies (and quite successfully), that Irish Spring soap makes you as clean as a mountain stream.

Once you have made your list of what your product is like (or if you can't think of anything), make another list of what your product is not like. Sometimes it is easier to figure out what you don't want as a solution. If you can't think of more than a few things that your product is like, look at the opposite list and try to think of the opposite of those things. Chances are that this back-and-forth comparison will eventually lead to a long list of creative springboards.

If rhymes, analogies, and synonyms are too constraining, try writing (or recording) in stream of consciousness. Psychologists use this technique to get to the heart of a problem. As a graphic designer you should also be able to find the heart of your communication problem. This is easy, and is restricted by virtually no rules. Write down the first thing that comes to mind when you think of your problem. Keep writing until you run out of thoughts. Let your mind wander in any direction, and don't try to constrain yourself by convention.

If your problem is to create a new logo for a computer company, what is the first thought that comes to mind when you think of computers? Write down each thought that comes to mind about computers, and see where your creative mind leads you. Of course, this does not mean that you have a final solution when you reach "hippopotamus"; some streams may veer a bit from the desired path. But look back through your list and think of *how* you got from one thing to the next. You may even find that certain items lead into their own streams of consciousness. Let these ideas flow freely. By the time you're completely out of ideas, you should have a long list of thoughts that will help you create a great solution to the original problem.

Regardless of the specific project on which you're working, word play can lead to new and creative design solutions. There is always more than one way to say the same thing. Look for alternative words when looking for a new idea.

The following example describes how word games can lead to effective and creative solutions. Granby Colorado Disposal Company (what a boring name!) wanted to reinvent themselves. Brainstorming started by listing all the words that could substitute for "garbage" in the name of the disposal service; in another column on the same page, all the ways to dispose of household garbage were listed:

Waste	Burn
Sanitation	Incinerate
Swill	Removal Service
Refuse	Garbage Heap
Rubbish	Dump
Debris	Burn
Trash	Cremate
Scum	Incinerate
Dustbin	Disappear
Incinerator Food	Zap!
Raw Fuel	Abracadabra! Poof!
Maggoty Fodder	Presto!
Recyclables	

Something about "Zap!" was exciting — the way the letters Z-a-p looked in a cartoon typeface. That led to thinking about cartoon symbols to illustrate the concept "Zap!", which led to lightning bolts. This led to a brainstorm of all the ways to say lightning.

Bolt
Jaggedy
Flash

Flash rhymes with trash, which is on the original list... *Flash Trash — You Wrap It, We Zap It!* was born.

The company trucks were all painted navy blue with a huge yellow lightning bolt on the sides, the trash collectors all wore blue jumpsuits emblazoned with a lightning bolt across the back, and the complimentary trash bags the customers used were navy with the signature yellow lightning bolt. Granby Colorado Disposal Company was reinvented.

Visual Brainstorming

Brainstorming, for graphic designers and other two-dimensional artists, is more often than not, a visual process. We generally think in terms of images rather than words. Many of us perform better at brainstorming with thumbnail sketches.

When we are assigned a particular project, we try to come up with visual solutions by scribbling quick and dirty sketches in our sketchbooks, on scrap paper, the utility bill envelope — any available blank piece of paper. This is a good reason to always have a sketchbook with you. Once you've filled a book, keep it accessible as part of your inspirational file. Ask any designer who has been working in the field for a while, and they'll probably have a small library of these books.

Like word games, scribble any idea that comes to mind. Don't worry about rendering perfect shading or exact perspective;

by A.M. Giraldo

Examples of visual brainstorming (top), and the final Corporate ID package.

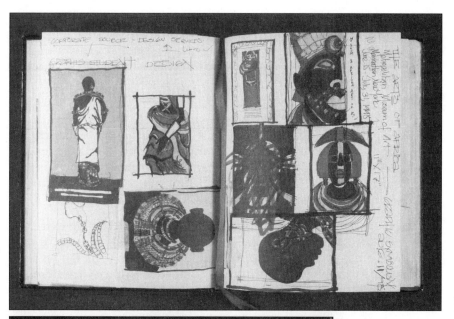

by A.M. Giraldo

Examples of visual brainstorming (top) for an art show poster, and the final proof based on the thumbnails.

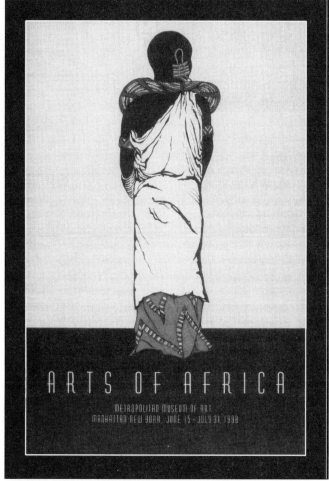

this stage is only dealing with concepts. Remember that you want to present your client with options solve the problem, but the concept stage does not have to be a final design. You don't want to spend hours working on a finalized image that will eventually be thrown away.

Dealing with Creative Block

Every designer and artist, during at least one point in his or her career, will experience creative block. In fact, many seasoned designers expect some level of creative block at the beginning of any new project. We get a new project, stare at a blank piece of paper (or our computer monitor, or a pristine new canvas) and have no idea what to do.

We all get stuck for ideas. You've tried all of the brainstorming exercises, and you still feel like you couldn't come up with a good idea to save your life. Creative block can be paralyzing, especially when your job revolves around your creativity. Following are some well-known symptoms of creative block, and suggestions for getting past it.

RATIONALIZATION

"I'm bored" or "I don't feel like it" or "I'm not interested." If you find yourself saying this type of thing, you may be in creative-block denial. Find one small aspect of the problem and focus on that, perhaps a technical point or background research. The important point is to keep at it, even if it is just a small aspect of the work.

PROCRASTINATION

Procrastination is deadly because we can honestly rationalize that we have plenty of time to come up with a concept and produce the job. Many designers claim that they work best under pressure... a great excuse to wait until the last minute to start a project.

Maybe you do work well under pressure, but waiting until the last minute only creates even bigger limitations to what you can create. How can you know how long a job will take if you don't know what the job will entail? If you put off the concept stage of a design project, you may find that you don't have enough time to hold a photo shoot, find the right materials, or whatever else might be involved in production. And even if your last-minute concept is the best design ever, it doesn't matter a bit if there's no time left to execute it.

Procrastination is frequently a cover for lack of focus. Once you admit that you're procrastinating, it's an easy problem to overcome. If your design solution requires a long-range deadline, break up the work into more short-term goals. Shorter, tighter deadlines keep you focused. Short-term goals will also help give you a sense of accomplishment and progress.

BURN OUT

If you've been working on the same project for a while, or have been working long hours for a long time, you may eventually burn out. There is simply no energy left to develop new creative ideas. When you reach this point, progress stops dead in its tracks.

Re-evaluate your goals. What was the original problem? If you have absolutely no idea how to solve it, chances are you are not looking at the real problem. Go back to the very basics of brainstorming.

Are there non-creative tasks that can be delegated to other people while you work on creative concepts? Are there other people who can provide creative input? If you have reached burnout, you may find it helpful to collaborate, not only to lighten your workload but also to infuse new creative juices into your design.

OVERWORK

If you find yourself overwhelmed, overworked, or overstressed, you will probably hit a creative wall more often than usual. Some people perform well under pressure; their creativity relies on staying close to a nervous breakdown. If, however, pressure is not your friend, find a way to break up the pressure. Do something that you find to be calming... anything that takes your mind off of your workload. Most designers have a

physical or mental release that refreshes the creative juices. When stress becomes too much to handle, go back to your comfort zone for a while until the walls aren't closing in.

"I'M NOT A CREATIVE PERSON."

This can be a self-fulfilling prophecy. Remember that creativity is a skill that should be nurtured. If you stop treating yourself as a creative person, your creative skill will wilt. Once you have decided that you are not creative, you will expect and accept less from your creative mind.

If you think your designs are stupid, weak, trite, or boring, you've hit yet another creative wall. But stupid, weak, and trite ideas are necessary to the creative process. Remember that you're human — the first psychological reaction to any problem is usually something we've seen or done before. Don't get discouraged if your first ideas are cliche. Instead, use those concepts as the beginning of a stream of consciousness. Where does your mind lead from these "same-old-thing" solutions?

Also keep in mind that there *aren't* any stupid ideas. You don't have to use these concepts as your final solution. Take a step back, and use your "boring" ideas as the basis for a new brainstorm — try juxtaposing ideas or opposites.

CHAPTER 3

Abstraction, Symbolism, and Visual Metaphor

Art is a lie that leads us to the truth.

—PABLO PICASSO

Abstraction

Abstraction is the systematic reduction of a detailed visual idea to its most essential, recognizable lines, shape, or essence.

A photograph, line drawing, or painting are low levels of abstractions, because they don't reduce the level of representation by much. As an example, we find low levels of abstraction with a realistic landscape oil painting. Every detail is painstakingly painted in — each blade of grass, the birds in the tree, the rocks edging a gurgling stream. A deeper level of abstraction (reduction) is apparent in the works of Impressionist painters. Their

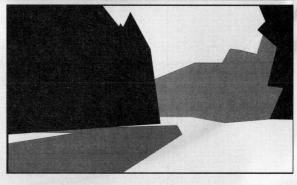

An image (top) can be abstracted to give only the impression of the scene (middle), or even to show only the most basic elements. The same principle applies to design — pay attention to the overall composition of your design, including the basic shapes of the elements.

landscapes are recognizable as landscapes, even without every blade of grass; their intention was to give you the impression (hence the name) of the scene. The landscape might be further abstracted by using only the paint colors and the actual brush strokes to convey that particular landscape on that particular day.

Fashion photography, in particular, uses abstraction all the time to sell clothes, cosmetics, and perfume. Picture the model in the foreground; the background is hazy and unfocused to give only a hint of the photo location. The viewer has the essence of where the scene was shot, and is free to interpolate a specific place that would be individually pleasing. The most important thing about perfume is the way it makes a woman feel; this kind of abstraction allows the viewer to focus on the imagery or the fantasies that the fragrance represents. The visual solution is created by abstracting the essence of the perfume's promise.

Graphic designers can use the theory of abstraction when trying to solve a visual problem. Think of the essence of what you are trying to design. Reduce your problem to the fewest lines that can represent the heart of your idea.

Symbolism and the Visual Metaphor

A symbol is a visual metaphor that we have come to use interchangeably with an idea or concept. We use symbols as a type of visual shorthand to quickly convey ideas or concepts. They are a reliable "language" in all visual arts and every designer should become a collector of symbols that have become integrated into ads, Web design, and other visual venues.

We are exposed to symbols every day, even if you don't consciously realize it. How many of these do you recognize?

HOW ARE SYMBOLS USED?

Not too long ago, graphic storytelling was necessary to communicate with a largely illiterate population. People relied on paintings and drawings to tell stories and record history. Beginning with early Man, cave drawings give us some record of what took place thousands of years ago. Of course you cannot make a 700-page painting, so events had to be condensed into symbolic images. Medieval and Renaissance art give us many very sophisticated examples of this type of visual communication.

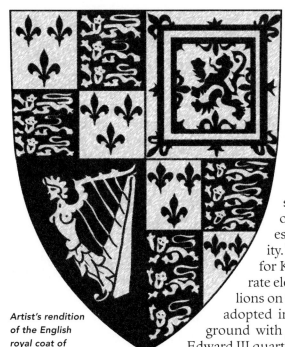

Artist's rendition of the English royal coat of arms for James I (1603).

The image shown here provides an excellent example of how images were used as symbols. Unless you've studied medieval English history, you probably wouldn't recognize this symbol of King James I of England. But you can bet that any of the king's contemporaries would have instantly known who was riding across the countryside if this image was embroidered on a banner.

Heraldry (the kind of identity crest shown on the left) is a highly artistic form of symbolism. These crests were used to establish identity, ownership, and heredity. The entire image is a symbol, in this case for King James I of England. But every separate element of the crest is also a symbol. Three lions on the dark background represent England, adopted in 1195 by Richard I. The white background with *fleur-de-lis* represents France. In 1340, Edward III quartered the fleur-de-lis field with England's three lions, symbolizing his claim to the thrones of both countries. The royal crest was again quartered in 1603 when James VI of Scotland became King James I of England; the bottom left quarter is the symbol of Ireland, the top right quarter symbolizes Scotland. Adding each of these elements to one shield means that this image not only symbolized the person of James I, but also symbolized a "united kingdom" (this term was not yet in use) of England, France, Scotland, and Ireland.

You might even further break down the specific elements of this crest. The lion, fleur-de-lis, harp, and other specific icons all had symbolic meaning during the medieval period. Our intention here, though, is not to present a dissertation on medieval symbolism. Of course we no longer ride on horseback across a battlefield, or need to use images to proclaim identity to a largely illiterate population.

MODERN SYMBOLISM

Symbolism has evolved over time with culture. Since written literacy has increased, modern society relies less and less on visual images to communicate ideas. But modern symbolism is no less complex, no less sophisticated; it is simply different.

In the very simplest sense, symbols are easily recognizable elements that convey specific meaning. You probably didn't recognize the image on the previous page as King James I of England. But can you think of a symbol for the American president (whether Republican or Democrat)?

Modern society has a highly developed visual language. There are still easily recognizable images, but today those symbols tend to be in the form of corporate logos. Chances are you know what the Nike "swoosh" looks like, even if it doesn't say Nike. The next time you are watching TV, notice the products that characters use; the logos of popular

companies are slightly changed because of fees for licensing. But you probably still associate the red and white cola can with Coca Cola, or the blue laptop with a white circle on the front as an Apple iBook. Successful corporate brand design relies on the ability to plant these images in the consumer mind as easily recognizable symbols, even when they are abstracted to the most basic element.

Propaganda and Motivational Psychology

Symbolism in modern design has moved from specific item association to conceptual relation. We use an entire composition to convey a feeling or emotion. The trick is to create a visual image of something your audience desires. Think of what your audience hopes to gain by using the product you are advertising. Wealth, beauty, power, prestige, social status, fame, and popularity are all powerful motivators for virtually any person.

People often buy things to satisfy emotional needs rather than physical ones. Abraham Maslow, a famous psychologist, researched and listed a hierarchy of human needs. Humans rank the most important basic needs:

1. Survival (sex is associated with racial survival
2. Security (personal and family safety)
3. Community (social and peer approval)

Advertising is filled with subtle (and not-so-subtle) cues designed to motivate and influence consumers; the viewing audience may not even realize that they are being influenced.

For example, an ad shows a well-groomed young man in a tuxedo, sipping wine while standing in a ballroom with shining chandeliers. The visual metaphors in this ad tell us exactly who the man is. His hairstyle is flawless, the tie is perfectly tied, the wine glass is expensive crystal; all factors that suggest polish and taste. The large room has a marble floor and shimmering crystal chandeliers — not your average living room. Every image in the ad conveys wealth, taste, and prestige. The idea is that if we buy this wine, we will be able to stand in the same elegant setting with this tastefully dressed man — we will be elevated to a prestigious (and envious) status. You may think that people are not this naive but they are: the advertising works.

As a society we react to and translate many visual metaphors. We know that the man in black jeans and a motorcycle jacket is not the good guy. We perceive a white plastic radio to be cheaper (and therefore less prestigious) than a black-and-chrome radio. A birthday card with daisies is for a little girl, not for a boy. Successful design centers on these typical psychological responses to emotional cues; your job as a designer is to visually communicate those cues. The more help you give your message, the more successful your design will be.

VISUAL OVERLOAD

Every day we are bombarded with TV and print ads, Internet graphics, billboards, movies, and junk mail — all brightly colored, symbol-laden, attention-grabbing. The demands for fresh, innovative, never-been-done-before imagery is high because we tend to bore easily. In an era of instant gratification and sensory overload, most people won't take time to examine an image that they have already seen before.

ICONS

Icons are graphic symbols designed to quickly convey information in a stylized, abstracted manner. Icons should be universally understandable, since they are quickly becoming the standard "world language." Icons are used frequently in the travel and tourism industry, the transportation industry, for international sporting events, and for merchandising.

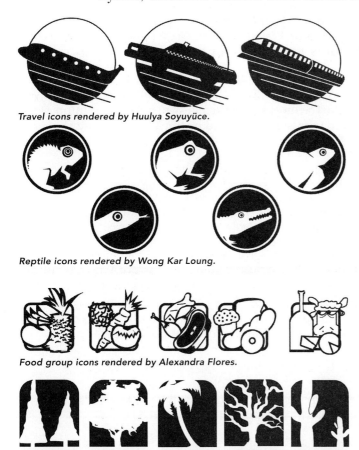

Travel icons rendered by Huulya Soyuyüce.

Reptile icons rendered by Wong Kar Loung.

Food group icons rendered by Alexandra Flores.

Icon design has three main considerations. First, they must work in black and white (or only one color, since most signs are printed this way). Successful icons make good use of the interaction between positive and negative space instead of relying on detailed color rendering. Second, an icon should work equally well large (for example, on an airport sign) and small (on a travel brochure). Finally, icons should be bold and simple so that they can be universally interpreted.

Using rounded edges helps to contain the visual energy of an icon. These tree icons (by Chris Morris) incorporate excellent negative/positive space interaction within the rounded boundary.

Dealing with the Cliché

Imagery seen too often is often not seen at all. This is the case with over-used design symbols and everyday objects. Overuse renders them ineffective, and they lose their power to communicate.

"It is the function of the designer to revitalize these cliched symbols and objects by interpreting them in individual and personal ways." This is a direct quote from Richard Wilde, former Chairman of the Graphic Design and School of Visual Arts, from his book *Problems: Solutions, Visual Thinking for Graphic Communicators*, VanNostrand Reinhold Company, N.Y.

 Everyone knows what the symbol of a heart implies. People don't really see the heart; the heart shape and red color lead to a shorthand synaptic response: Love.

When dealing with symbols and visual language, you have to:

• Get the audience's attention

• Keep the audience's attention

• Communicate your intention to the audience

This is asking a lot, but it is not impossible. This is one excellent reason why you should never settle for the first few symbolic "answers" that you think of during brainstorming. Write them down, purge your mind of the trite symbols used to represent ideas, and be free to move on to the more creative answers.

Color Symbolism

In the visual world, color is the single most powerful symbolic tool at your disposal. Understanding and effectively using color as a symbolic or motivational tool is key to strong visual communication.

Color symbolism does vary from culture to culture, but Western culture generally associates certain colors with certain traits or attributes. The following is a short list of the symbolic meaning most frequently attached to certain colors. For further information, comprehensive sources of color symbolism are available in your library or local bookstore.

WHITE

White, the sum of all colors, is most commonly seen to represent purity or cleanliness. Consider these "colored" analogies:

Pure as the driven snow
Pure white
Angelic white gown
White wedding

White suggests unblemished purity — an immaculate canvas or a perfectly starched shirt; goodness — the good guy always wears white; and innocence — before anything has "sullied" the pure white.

White also represents the *void*, or a lack of anything at all. The Arctic Tundra, a barren and uninhabitable expanse of land, is perceived as white (even though in reality not every square inch of it is). The Ice Queen from childhood fairy tales is another example of white's negative symbolism. White, in this case, suggests bitterness, meanness, relentlessness. Jack Frost, another fictional character usually portrayed in white, suggests coldness and hardness.

YELLOW

Yellow can be a complicated color because of its different effects on a viewer. People associate yellow with warmth (the sun), happiness, spring, and youth. Yellow is all of this, yet it is even more.

The human eye processes yellow faster than any other color. Many companies that want to be associated with fast service use yellow predominantly. Western Union's logo is yellow and black; you can send money anywhere quickly. Taxi cabs are yellow—fast transportation. Midas and Meineke, two national auto services, have yellow identities—fast service.

Yellow also suggests danger. Yellow road signs warn you that the road might be slippery, that you should slow down, or that pedestrians are crossing. Even nature used yellow as a danger sign: yellow bees sting, yellow and black spiders bite, and yellow foliage might be poisonous.

Yellow takes the most human synaptic chemicals to process. People get irritated most frequently when yellow fills their field of view. Use yellow sparingly. Use it as an accent but never as a background. A little yellow goes a long way in making your point.

GREEN

Grass, plants, trees, and other natural organisms are brilliant green when they are alive. Green suggests freshness or new life, and is widely used to represent healing. Green has been a symbol of nature for centuries, as far back as the Green Man (the nature god) in ancient Celtic culture.

In the United States, our money is printed with green ink. Green, then, has come to symbolize wealth (and the negative aspects of wealth, greed and jealousy). Other cultures may not have green money, but they are aware of this color symbolism. Green as a symbol of jealousy long predates U.S. currency; Shakespeare warned to "beware, my lord, of jealousy; it is the green-ey'd monster..."

RED

Red is the color of passion, fire, heat, anger, and "true love." It is a very exciting, confident color. Use it to make a bold statement. Red used in its clear, middle values symbolizes strength. Darker, more moody shades represent rage, hatred, blood, battles, and war.

PURPLE

Dark shades of purple suggest royalty, and are sometimes used to signify wisdom. Middle shades of purple might be considered artsy and flamboyant. Care should be taken when using this color, both because of the rather contradictory symbolistic meanings and because it is very gender specific. You should not use purple when trying to communicate a "macho" message — some men perceive purple as a "women's color."

PINK

Certainly, pink is seen as a little girl's color. It can also be used effectively to represent a heart freely given, such as the love of a parent for a child or between family members. Pink is also used to enhance the sense of sweetness, which is why bakery goods are so often packaged in pink boxes. Pink also suggests a greater value for goods or services packaged with the color (the proverbial "rose-tinted glasses" effect).

BLUE

The symbolic meaning of blue also depends on the value and saturation of the hue. A light, clear blue encourages a feeling of airiness and fantasy.

Do you ever get The Blues? This is just an expression, but too much blue — such as blue text on blue paper with blue line art — can definitely have a depressing effect. Never use blue as the only color in a design unless you want the viewer to think of something dreary.

Medium shades of blue, called "professional blues", are frequently used as a background for political figures to enhance their veracity, traditional conservative values, their honesty, and steadfastness. The term "blue-blood" has long been used to imply loyalty and patriotism. Why? Our bodies pump more endorphins in the presence of blue, making us feel better. We think we feel better because we trust the politician.

Dark blues are considered professional and serious. The power suit in your closet is likely one of two colors—black or dark blue. In a professional setting, you would not merit the same consideration if you wore bright orange. Dark blue is also associated with spiritualism.

BLACK

Obviously, black is a symbol of death and mourning. We wear black to funerals (never to a wedding) and hang a black wreath on the door. The Black Death was one of the worst plagues ever to devastate Europe. Death personified (the Grim Reaper) almost always wears a voluminous black cloak.

Black also symbolizes danger or evil. Witches wear black, and have black cats; black widows are very poisonous spiders. Blackbeard, the Black Knight, and Black Bart are just a few examples of black's notorious association.

In addition to the negative symbolism, black is considered the most minimal, sophisticated color. Reversed type (white lettering on a black background) is seen as more costly and valued than the same message delivered as black type on white paper. Art rendered on a completely black board is perceived as infinitely more stylish and elegant than on a white page. We attend "black tie" events in black gowns and tuxedos. Use black when you want to increase the perceived value of a product.

GREY

Grey is the most attractive color to creative people. We work well and feel good in a grey environment. We adore the subtle elegance of grey on grey.

Grey, however, has powerful negative symbolism. Working class people associate grey with industrial uniforms and react negatively to it. People who live in wet, rainy areas (such as London or Seattle) perceive the color as very dreary and also react negatively to it.

Do you realize that a major factor in client approval for your design job is whether you get the color right? Everything else about the job can be correct, but if the colors are wrong then the whole thing is wrong. With this in mind, we are certain you will spend somewhat more time choosing exactly the right color palette for your next design job.

Summing It All Up

Refining your skill in visual literacy is mostly training your awareness. It takes practice — getting into a habit of analyzing the posters, paintings, CD covers, food packages, ads, and all of the designed work you see.

This is an ongoing adventure — symbolism is an evolving entity. Just look at the illustrations of the 1950s and you will quickly see how cultural iconography and symbolism have changed. Recognizing and using culturally-developed symbolic references is a matter of paying attention.

CHAPTER 4

Putting It All Together

All things began in order, so shall they end,
and so shall they begin again.

—Sir Thomas Browne

The Production Process

Once you have a brilliant concept (or at least a solid idea), the big question is: "Where do we go from here?" How do you get the idea from the initial, very loose thumbnail to a workable, finished solution? A very structured series of steps exists that take you smoothly from your initial concept to the pressrun. The steps are, in order:

1. Thumbnails

2. Roughs

3. Proof

4. Printing

Once all the brainstorming is completed, your design problem should encompass many suggestions. First you need to eliminate the obviously impossible choices. Some ideas won't work because they are too expensive to produce. Others will work only at very large sizes, and you need a more versatile solution. Still others won't work because they require a different medium, and you have to work with only paper and ink. Get the idea? Know the specifics for your final product, and narrow your design choices. Once you've eliminated physical impossibilities, consider your target market. Some approaches will work well for certain markets, but will fall flat in others.

Be specific in your marketing approach. From the remaining choices, select the most workable concept.

THUMBNAILS

Once you have your design idea, create *thumbnail sketches* of different possibilities for that idea; this is a kind of visual brainstorming but with a more narrow focus. You aren't looking for any possible idea anymore, only ways to depict the idea you've already chosen. Keep the content in mind, and sketch ideas that best convey your intended message.

by A.M. Giraldo

Several thumbnail sketches (above) designed to get an idea for an ad, and the rough based on those thumbnails (left).

ROUGHS

Once your thumbnails are created, the idea moves into the rough stage of design. A *rough* is full-size rendition of your design, and in many cases incorporates elements from several different thumbnails. You (or your client, if you've presented the thumbnails for review) may decide that you like the type in one thumbnail, the layout in another, and the images from yet another.

The main purpose of the rough is to show what the elements look like rendered at the actual size of the piece. Relationships are frequently distorted in tiny sketches: type and illustrations look much different and disproportionate when sketched at small sizes. Once an idea is rendered full size, it is obvious if a typeface will work, or if the overall composition is weak.

Some designers create everything on a computer, including these early stages of an idea. If this is the case, your "roughs" will not look very rough at all. Other designers insist on using traditional media (such as markers, pastels, and pencils) for the rough stage so that the client will not

consider this to be a finalized version of the piece. Keep in mind that if you use traditional media to create the roughs, you will eventually have to create the final piece either digitally or as camera-ready art.

(Below) A rough of an ad idea.

(Right) The same idea taken to the next level — the rough.

by A.M. Giraldo

PROOF

The goal of the proofing process (generically called "proofing" throughout the industry) is to guarantee exactly what your design will look like when it is printed. The proof should also show any folding, embossing, cutting, or other special requirements.

There are many different types of proofs available. Depending on your specific project needs, one proof may be more appropriate than another. High-end color proofs are made from the same files that will be used for printing; different proofing systems have different color and resolution capabilities. You should ask your printer for a color proof, which will either be created from film or directly from the files.

Check your proof carefully against your copy of the job: closely compare the text, colors, and images to make sure that nothing got lost in the move. Once you are satisfied that the proof is what you expected, present it to your client for the same inspection. Make sure the client signs and dates the proof. No job should ever be printed without the client's signature. Once you have the client's signature, you shouldn't be blamed if

1.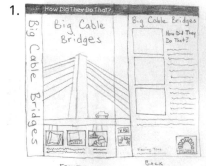

The three stages of the design process:

1. A thumbnail sketch gave the client an idea what elements would be on the box, and where each would be placed.

2. The rough, in this case, was created electronically. The designer is able to use the actual elements — photos, fonts, and artwork — that will eventually be printed. This kind of rough eliminates the guesswork that traditional media introduces.

3. The final proof created from the electronic "rough." It is folded and assembled so the printing and production crews will know exactly what the final piece should look like.

by Liesel Donaldson

2.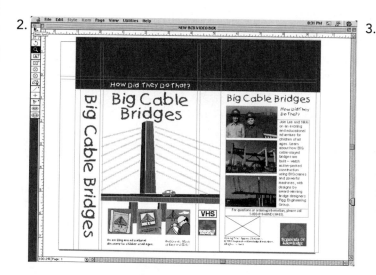

3.

a mistake is found later. (This does not give you license to be careless, but it provides some protection if the client later refuses to pay.)

Many jobs are printed with errors because of carelessness or because the project is behind schedule and you are forced to "just glance" at the proof. One printing company printed its own posters with an incorrect phone number because everyone simply assumed it was correct. No one noticed the wrong area code until 5,000 copies of the six-color poster were done. A publisher printed a book cover with its own name spelled incorrectly on the front cover. The book was bound and sent to the distribution house before anyone noticed that the 18-point name was wrong. The book had to be unbound, the cover reprinted, and then rebound at considerable expense.

Desktop inkjet printers are increasingly being used to proof non-color critical work (such as black-and-white newspaper ads). Small design groups find the consumables and hardware more practical than expensive, high-end color proofing systems. Keep in mind, an inkjet proof will not show accurate color. If your client approves an inkjet proof, make certain to explain that colors will be different (sometimes much different) on the final piece.

The second purpose of the proof is to provide instructions for press and finishing operators. The press operator looks at your proof and makes sure that the color being printed matches the color on your proof.

The mechanical nature of a printing press means that errors can appear even if the proof was correct. An experienced press operator will notice this kind of error before the job is finished, and will be able to correct the problem.

To help you organize the production process, we offer you one final creative strategy:

Chart Your Process

When confronted with a large design problem, it helps to make a large flowchart that highlights mini-deadlines. Tape a long piece of butcher paper to the wall (at least six feet in length). Use a permanent market to note the deadlines along a timeline.

Use this much paper so that you have lots of room for phone pad notes, rough drafts, Post-it®, brainstorm sheets, scribbled notes, cartoons, messages from other people, or anything else that might be relevant to the project.

Your flowchart works because you can see at a quick glance where you are in the project; Pantone color chips; project specifications; who you need to call when; and all necessary contact information (such as the printer's phone number and the copy editor's number). Everything is posted on the chart, so it doesn't get lost on a work table.

PROJECTS

The following projects are designed to apply the concepts you learned in Section 1: the creative thought process, verbal and visual brainstorming, designing with a specific audience in mind, and concept development. Each project correlates to an exercise in Section 2, where you will incorporate design elements into the ideas you generate.

These projects simulate "real-world" assignments.

Input from a client — "The Client Says."

Instructions from your art director — "Your Art Director Says."

A specific goal — "Your Final Submission."

You may choose to use a computer, but it is not necessary at this point.

A New Face on Sunny Island

THE CLIENT SAYS:

We just started phase three of our new exclusive resort on Sunny Island. We're about three months away from completion and we need to create a look that will attract the right kind of people. We're not a family vacation spot, and we don't have planned activities. We've decided to approach our guests with the idea of a week-long escape to luxury at our quiet, peaceful oceanside resort. This is the place you would go to lounge by the water and read, sleep, and just relax.

Everything is subtle, no garish floral theme or loud bands playing every night like so many other resorts. Our staff will be at the guests' beck and call, but they've been trained to blend into the background so that they don't interfere with the guests' complete relaxation. We've contracted the finest chefs, and we've got a well-stocked private wine cellar with nothing but the best. Our goal is to be able to provide anything the guest wants within minutes.

We need to name the place, something that gets our point across. We want a logo that instantly says "nothing but luxury." We've toyed with some ideas but we don't want to say anything about "paradise" or "relax" since every other resort already does that. We're spending a lot of money to make the resort perfect, and the identity needs to reflect that. What can you come up with?

YOUR ART DIRECTOR SAYS:

O.K., the client hasn't told us much, other than what they don't want. What other words can we use in place of "relax" and "paradise"? That's the first place to start.

I like the idea of subtle, so we can play with that. Of course, you can't use the same word over and over, so what else says the same thing? We also know that they've shunned "garish" colors, so stick to softer shades when you sketch the logos.

Since they used the words "the right kind of people," we can safely assume that we're not designing for the average tourist on this project. We also know that this place is going to cater to the wealthy, since they've got the "finest chefs... and a well-stocked private wine cellar." What can we assume about the intended demographic, and how do we communicate the subtle luxury idea?

I want you to create three possible identities for the resort — names, slogans, and logo ideas. We know they're opening in three months, so we don't have much time. Once the identity is developed, we'll have to incorporate that into advertising and promotional materials. The planning, design, and printing for that phase will take a while, so you have about two weeks to finish your ideas.

We can guess that these people are going to be very picky since they told us everything they don't like, so make sure you can defend what you create.

YOUR FINAL SUBMISSION:

Create three separate identities for the resort. Have three possible names, slogans, and at least five logo sketches for each name.

Reinventing the Zoo

THE CLIENT SAYS:

We're planning our grand reopening of the old City Zoo. We've finally moved into modern times, gotten rid of all the cages, and created realistic habitats for the animals. Our main goal now is rehabilitation, preservation, and education.

We want a new name and logo that invites people to learn more about the animals in our care. We're going to have educational programs and exhibits throughout the facility. But we *don't* want people to be scared off by the idea of learning! We've hired consultants to create everything to be both informational and fun, and we've gotten grants from the government and from private donors. They're all expecting something special, something wonderful... and we intend to give it to them.

We also need a series of icons to use throughout the park as direction signs. We're planning on a lot of international visitors, so we can't use any one language. The six main sections of the facility are: the tropics, the desert, the arctic, the forest, the ocean, and the sky. There will also be a special children's section, which also needs an icon.

We've submitted this project to two other design groups, and whichever group submits the best work will get our entire advertising contract. We'd like to see your ideas three weeks from today.

YOUR ART DIRECTOR SAYS:

The first thing we know is that we have three weeks to create a name, logo, and seven icons for the zoo.

Start with the name. We know their goals, but we don't want to use the tired "to protect and learn" phrasing. Think of different ways to say these things. While you're thinking of the words, try to keep in mind which words will lend themselves to visual depiction.

Once you've got the name in mind, come up with five different logo sketches. What colors would be the most inviting to a very general and international audience? Stay away from the cliched animal montage surrounding the name, since practically every zoo in the world uses that. And try not to use too much green, since that's the same color the City Zoo used to use in all their ads. We want to entirely reinvent the place.

After you've got your logo ideas, move on to the icons for the different sections of the facility. Create three different series so that we can present the clients with a choice. We want them to feel like we're inviting their input, even while we're doing our jobs. This could be a big contract for us, so make sure your logos, icons, and ideas are in a relatively finalized format — no simple sketches.

YOUR FINAL SUBMISSION:

Rename the zoo. Develop five comprehensive mechanicals of different logos, and three series of icons for the different sections of the zoo.

So Long, Crazy Harry

THE CLIENT SAYS:

We just purchased Crazy Harry's Used Car Dealership. You've probably seen the ads in the newspaper, with giant cartoon letters and pictures of circus animals. We want to reinvent the entire company as something a bit more sophisticated. We prefer to think of these cars as "preowned" instead of "used," and we'd rather not have any similarity to Harry's giant red starburst logo. We really like the way major dealerships promote full warranty and service customer care even when buying a "preowned" car. We need a slogan to help reinvent the lot's identity, and then another one to use as a permanent slogan. We'd like to announce the new ownership in two weeks. Can you help us?

YOUR ART DIRECTOR SAYS:

Let's break this down into chunks. First, we know that the client wants an entirely new identity, which means a new company name. What will be effective without simply using the owner's name? See what you can brainstorm into a workable idea.

We can make a few assumptions about the target market: First, these are people with limited resources, since they're not buying a new Mercedes from this dealership. We also know that the dealership is in the local suburbs, so we can guess that the average buyer might be interested in value and reliability. Can we infer anything else about what might be important to these buyers?

We know the client has an extremely short deadline; fortunately they're not looking for full advertisements right now. I want you to create three different identities for the dealership. When you have three possible names, work on the slogans. Remember, they need two different catch phrases — one to introduce the dealership to the public, and one to use as a permanent reminder. Finally, sketch a few logo thumbnails for each name. You might want to work a slogan right into the logo, but it's not necessary.

They didn't give us a lot of information about what they specifically want or don't want, which means that they're going to be open to suggestion. As long as you can defend what you create, we should be able to sell one of your ideas.

YOUR FINAL SUBMISSION:

You will develop three separate identities for the auto dealership.

For each name, you should have an introductory slogan and three possible identity slogans.

For each name, you should also have 5 to 10 thumbnail sketches for logos.

SECTION 2

USING THE ELEMENTS

In Section 1 you learned that you do not need to be Picasso to develop a creative and effective visual solution to a design problem. It bears repeating that good graphic design is not the same thing as art; creativity is a skill that can be learned through practice. Similarly, the physical elements of graphic design can be mastered. The ability to paint a perfect sunset or draw a perfect rose is not as important as the ability to use the elements of design to solve your communication problem.

A carpenter builds with a hammer and nails; you build with lines, shapes, colors, type, and pictures. The carpenter knows when a bolt is more effective than a nail; you should know when red is more appropriate than yellow, when a photo works better than a drawing, when that photo belongs in a specific place. The carpenter also knows that the frame has to be sturdy enough to support the house; as a designer, you should know how to create a frame that supports your design. For every design problem, you are trying to communicate something; the physical elements of design are your tools of communication.

Look through a magazine about any topic that interests you. Rip out all the ads and place them side by side. You'll see numerous designs created by many different people, and by using ads from the same magazine, you will be looking at a handful of ads all created for the same target market. Stand far enough away from the ads so that you can no longer read any of the words. Look at the shapes, lines, colors, and the placement of the elements on the pages. Remove the ads that you don't like, for whatever reason, and put them into a separate pile.

With a few specific exceptions, it is not our intention to give you a list of rules... "You must place this red line in this space and in this direction." Rather, this section introduces the physical elements of design, and offers suggestions and ideas that will help you use the elements effectively.

As you read through the chapters in Section 2, go back to your two groups of ads and see if you can identify the elements that make some ads work and others not. How is the concept of line used to move your eye to the important part of a message? Why does a red headline work for one ad, but not for another? Why do some ads fill every millimeter of space on the page, and others are better with large "empty" areas? How are pictures used (and misused) to convey the advertiser's message? How does the type work (or not work) within each ad?

One of the best ways to master these concepts is to keep those questions in mind for everything you see. One designer commented that after years of this constant critique, she has to look at everything twice... first to evaluate the design and second to read the content. You will find that as you become more familiar with the elements, you'll be able to use them effectively and creatively in your design work.

Remember the questions you asked in Section 1. Once you've completed a design project, ask the same questions, this time with an eye to the physical elements:

- Does the design answer your specific problem or goal?

- Is the design creative and original?

- Is the design an appropriate treatment for the intended media?

- Will the design work within the budget?

- Is the style appropriate for the client and the target audience?

- Is the style appropriate for the intended message?

- Is your client happy with the job?

CHAPTER 5

Shape/Container Relationship

The note I handle no better than any other pianist. But the pauses between the notes — ah, that is where the art resides!

— SCHNABEL, COMPOSER AND VIRTUOSO

Design is not simply marks on paper. Design is a partnership between creative thought and the two-dimensional elements that comprise the visual language. Understanding the visual language and "alphabet" of this medium is integral to creating a cogent, powerful visual statement, be it a letterhead design, a company newsletter, a local advertisement, or a sales presentation.

The size and visual weight of the elements convey the meaning of your message; in addition, your communication is affected by the page's shape (format), as well as by where the elements are placed on that page. Before exploring the design elements themselves, let's look at the foundational issue of how a mark, a shape, a line of type, or an illustration relates to the page — the *shape/container relationship*.

Looking at the Container

Most people are more concerned with the *contents* of an element (what the word says or what the picture is) than with the placement of that element. But the position of that element in relationship to the page itself has tremendous influence on the perception of the message. Think of visual design as a purposeful arrangement of elements that reinforces or amplifies a theme, statement, or perception.

Most people are also affected by the *shape* of the container (the paper that is holding the visual element). Pick up a piece of standard 8.5 × 11-in. bond paper. It feels very normal. Now fold it in half vertically. It looks elegant, slim, pricey, understated. Unfold the paper, then fold it horizontally. Imagine receiving a flyer printed on this format. It feels squat and cheap, like someone was trying to save money by printing on half a sheet of paper.

This is a simple introduction to the effect that the dimensions of your paper can have on the perception of your message. Below are some examples of different paper containers. Can you think of a specific use for each format, and why it would work better than another for that purpose?

PLACING A SHAPE WITHIN THE CONTAINER

When asked to place an element on a page, the majority of people tend to place it in the middle of the top-third of the page. When asked to add another element of the same size and visual weight, it usually goes directly parallel to the first. When given three identical elements to place, people make a "face." Humans have a tendency to organize visual elements into some recognizable entity; a face is the most common. People repeatedly make this arrangement of shapes, rarely thinking of how the elements relate to the page itself.

An item's position on a page conveys unconscious, nearly subliminal messages. Is the image stable and centered? Do the images crowd the edge? Does the positioning feel top-heavy? Is it anchored firmly and unmovable? Does it appear light and able to fly off the page? Look at the illustrations to the right and process the shape/container relationship of each.

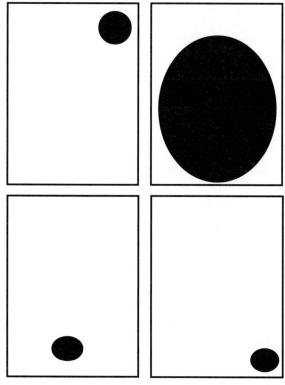

REAL-WORLD SHAPE/CONTAINER RELATIONSHIPS

In the real world of graphic design, a designer is asked to create an ad, brochure, flyer, or some other printed material to a specific size requirement. Then they are asked to rework the same ad (with the same copy, illustrations, and elements) into different sizes or "containers." The rough sketches shown here illustrate how changing the format also changes the look and feel of the printed message.

by A.M. Giraldo

Balance — Use of Space

The term *balance* refers to the arrangement of shapes, illustrations, and text on a page or within a publication. Some very specific guidelines govern the theories and practices of using this design principle.

THE THEORY FROM A DESIGNER'S VIEWPOINT

The idea of balance in graphic design is to arrange elements within a page or a layout so that the elements create a harmonious composition.

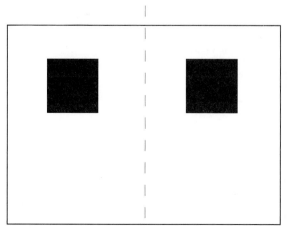

When we look at a page layout, we tend to see bilaterally (side-to-side). We mentally divide a page with an imaginary central vertical axis, creating a left side and a right side. If an element is placed within that page on the left side, we want to counterbalance it with a similar weight on the right side.

Example of a horizontal page balanced bilaterally. Can you think of a more interesting arrangement of the elements that would still appear balanced?

Types of Balance

There are three types of balance commonly used in graphic design: formal (symmetrical), informal (asymmetrical), and radial. Once you've read the following descriptions of balance, see if you can find examples of each type of balance in magazines, newspapers, or other design.

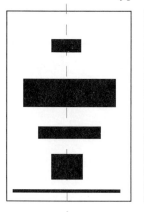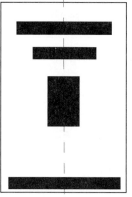

Formal balance is the arrangement of equally-weighted elements to the left and right of the center vertical axis (looks like a mirror image).

FORMAL (SYMMETRICAL) BALANCE

Formal balance is the placement of visual elements with equal distribution of visual weight on the left and right side of the imaginary center vertical axis. The left and right sides are mirror images. A centered line of type is an example of formal balance. Two illustrations of pages with formal balance are shown on the left.

How to Use Formal Balance.

Formal or symmetrical balance is used to give the appearance of solidity, stasis, integrity, tradition, longevity, permanence, and other dependable ideals. Companies that want to convey the image of reliability or trustworthiness are good candidates for formal balance. Insurance companies, financial consultants, and attorneys might all benefit from formal balance on their corporate stationery.

by A.M. Giraldo

Notice the symmetry of balance, and the seriousness and formality conveyed by its use.

INFORMAL (ASYMMETRICAL) BALANCE

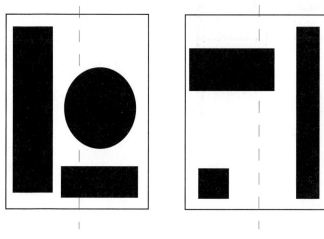

Informal balance is the asymmetrical arrangement of elements independent of the center vertical axis.

Informal balance is far more common than formal balance. Informal balance is the asymmetrical arrangement of elements within a page or layout; it does not rely on the centered effect to create a harmonious composition. The left and right sides of a page do not need to mirror each other, nor do they need to have the same elements. The idea is to imply balance by using elements that seemingly counterbalance each other. Informal balance is trickier to achieve than formal balance; take care using this method, and do not disregard the properties of the page.

How to Use Informal Balance. Informal or asymmetrical balance gives the appearance of modern, trendy, energetic, free-spirited, fresh, casual, and smart. A sports store, electronics company, Web design group, or fashion magazine might all use informal balance to good effect. A real-world example of this type of balance is shown below.

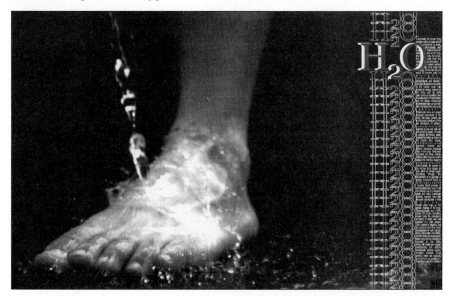

by K. Escheverria

Notice how the asymmetrical balance increases the dynamics and visual energy in this double-page magazine comp.

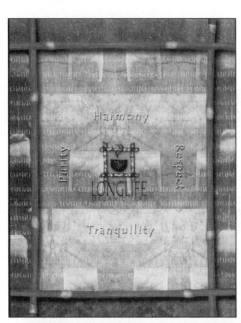

These examples illustrate two different balance treatments for the same promotional campaign. The asymmetrical (informal) balance gives a feeling of airiness and energy to the billboard

by A.M. Giraldo

(Left) The conservative, traditional, even stiff attitude of tea ceremonies is exemplified through the use of rigorous formal balance in the piece.

(Below) Billboard for the LongLife Tea Company uses informal balance.

RADIAL BALANCE

Radial balance is a variation on formal balance. It promotes all attributes connected with formal balance, but also reinforces the concept of equal partnership, teamwork, and unity. It is the arrangement of visual elements around a central point, like rays from the sun or the petals of a daisy.

This type of balance is the least likely to be used because it is dependent on the equal distribution of visual elements outward from a central axis. Think of the spokes of a bike wheel radiating from the center. Not many text or visual elements lend themselves to this type of arrangement. An illustration of radial balance is shown here.

How to Use Radial Balance. Radial balance is used to give the appearance of unity, working together, or separate-but-equal relationships. Potential usages of radial balance include a logo for a medical group, team of independent contractors, church group, or board of trustees. Use radial balance any time you want to give equal status or value to each element in the design.

by Mariel Hernandez

An example of radial balance. Notice how the longest word, "Remember,"
is balanced by the word "Dream" in a larger typeface.

Negative and Positive Space

Seasoned graphic designers are as acutely concerned with the negative space (empty areas) as they are with the positive space, or content of that page. One school of thought within design circles believes that empty space makes the statement, rather than what the words actually say.

THE THEORY FROM A DESIGNER'S VIEWPOINT

This idea of interaction between the page and its contents — the negative and positive relationship — is also referred to as the *figure/ground relationship*. People tend to see a subject as a dark shape against a white (or lighter) background. If the relationship is reversed (a black background with white shapes, or reversed type), the spatial relationships between the content and the page appear different, and are usually more visually energetic, lively, and modern.

Designers are concerned with the shape of the negative space as well as that of the positive items within the page. It takes practice to be able to discriminate between a sublime use of negative space and an awkward one.

What do you see? The vase or the two faces?

What do you see? The bird spreading its wings or the question mark?

The figure/ground relationship creates an illusionary third shape, which occurs because the mind is unable to discriminate between the subject and what is the background. The famous "vase or faces" illustration (shown left) demonstrates this interaction between the negative and positive space.

An equally intriguing illusion of negative and positive space is shown below the "vases or faces". This is part of a whole series of psychological experiments relating to the way most people structure visual information.

How to Use Negative and Positive Space.
Japanese ink drawings show an excruciating awareness of the harmony and integrity in sophisticated use of negative and positive space. It is a widely held Japanese design theory that there is only one perfect place on a canvas for a brush stroke, and it will speak to you if you "still your mind and listen." If that is too esoteric for you, an entire Western school of thought exists concerning negative space and what to fill it with. The phrase "less is more" best sums it up.

Remember that vast expanses of negative space do more to increase the air of luxury and elegance than any other visual tool. A blank page with a single line of small type seems to say, "We could afford to buy the whole page for our understated ad, just so we could avoid being on the same crowded page with other (perhaps competing) contents." The opposite is also true: a small, crowded ad with a zillion things all mashed into a 1-column space seems to say that the company is penny-pinching and stingy (or thrifty, or cost-conscious).

Three different versions of the same ad provide an example of how to use negative/positive space interaction. Which do you notice first in each ad, the t-shirt or the triangles?

This example uses three black triangles to create the t-shirt out of the negative space. The negative space is the most important element of the ad, "simply" depicting the message of the ad.

simply
Hanes

This example reverses the elements in the first version. Negative space is reduced to only the three small triangles and the text. This example is not as effective as the first, since the black space seems to overpower the text. The viewer may be overwhelmed by the large, solid black space.

simply
Hanes

simply
Hanes

This version uses the exact same shape as the first two ads. Though this example may seem exaggerated, many ads like it have appeared in the consumer market. The negative and positive space practically attack each other, and the original t-shirt shape is virtually unrecognizable. The viewer's eye moves with the path of the positive space, right and up, away from the message of the ad in the bottom corner.

CHAPTER 6

Layout

The concept of form — like poetry and religion, is a secret creation of the spirit... higher than function, materials or technique stands form.

— MUTHESIUS, VICE PRESIDENT OF THE WERKBUND

The arrangement of the visual elements on a page (or throughout the publication) is called the layout. A printing page setup might be referred to as the board or the flat, a remnant from the (not-so-distant) past when artwork was glued or pasted up on illustration boards in preparation for printing. This mechanical artwork is a very skilled craft that relies on the exact, clean placement of the many elements (text boxes, illustrations, captions, headlines, and so on) into the page design. The elements had to be painstakingly aligned by hand.

Desktop publishing software has largely replaced hand pasting (though you might still encounter a shop or two which still uses the traditional craft), but the arrangement of different elements still follows the same structure.

A foundational understanding of the standard sizes of formats available is important for any design project. A skilled graphic designer will first look to the standard formats and make all design decisions based on the choice of paper stock and format for that particular job.

Designing a layout a half-inch larger than standard size is a costly mistake that beginning designers make once. They find out quickly that the extra half inch involves the next larger paper size, which wastes space and could add hundreds of dollars to the production cost. We will discuss your paper and format options more in chapter 10, Paper, Binding, and Finishing.

Practically every aspect of design involves creating layouts. Whether you are creating a book with hundreds of pages, a one-page flyer, or a cellophane package, it is your job to arrange text, pictures, illustrations, and borders into a finished composition. This chapter will use simple illustrations to address layout concerns.

Use Master Pages to Design More Effectively

A *grid* is a layout template with defining guides for the margins, space between columns, and the space between a caption and an illustration. Every page within a publication should follow the same grid system, promoting coherence and unity throughout. Desktop publishing software allows you to easily create grids, or master pages, to use in your design projects.

Master pages leave little room for guesswork when you are working on a long document. Arrangement issues are solved when the template is created, making it much easier and faster to place the design elements throughout a job. Of course, an element can be misaligned on purpose to add visual interest and excitement to a project. However, if you misalign elements too frequently, the job will develop a chaotic, noncoherent look.

Layout Development

Layout design is a matter of composition. Chapter 5, Shape/Container Relationship discussed the placement of elements within a container. The issues discussed there are important points to remember once you begin your layout.

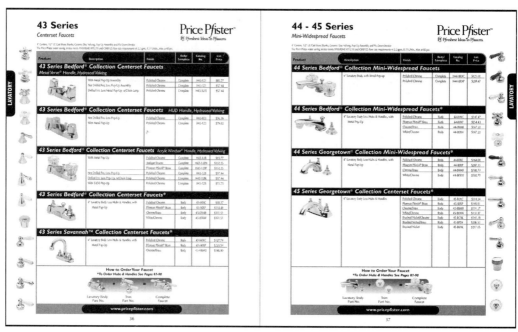

Courtesy Impress Communications

The column heading, "How to Order" information, category tab, page number, handle images, and headline structure are repeated (both position and style) on every page in a 120-page catalog. If each of these elements were placed by hand for every page of the catalog, you can plan on an extremely long layout session. You can also plan on mistakes — no matter how careful you are, you may forget the exact placement for an element, or simply enter a wrong number somewhere. Mistakes are human, and so are designers. (continued)

When you plan a layout, you shouldn't be working with specific elements. At the template stage, you should only be concerned with the kind of elements you'll eventually use. Is the project mostly text-based? Is it heavily illustrated? Is the project image-based, with only a few lines of type scattered throughout?

In this planning stage, you probably won't know what the final elements are going to be... the client didn't finish writing the text, the photographer hasn't submitted images, whatever the case may be. But you still have a deadline to meet, and the client wants to see your suggestions for a final layout. But even though you don't have the final elements, you know what they will be.

So that you can still create your layout ideas and meet your deadlines, designers have developed a system for faking it. You know that there will be images; use grey boxes as place holders until you get the actual images.

You know there will be an article of about 800 words. You have several options to mimic type for layout purposes. If you are developing your project on a computer, you can use *Greek type* as a place holder. Greeking comes in various typestyles, point sizes, and different column widths. Any company that sells typefaces and clip art will carry an extensive array of greeking. Some software ships with greeking in an "extras" folder. If you

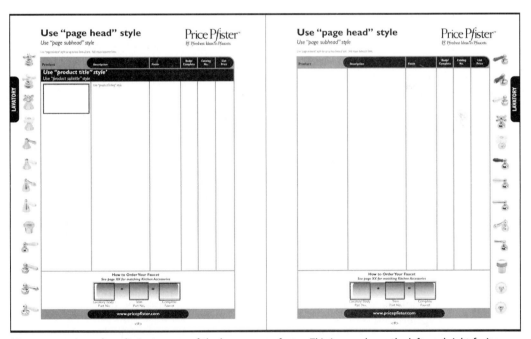

Master pages intend to eliminate some of the human error factor. This image shows the left- and right-facing master pages used to create the catalog layout shown on page 54; the master pages include the elements common to all pages; orange boxes mark the image place holders. Another useful feature of master pages is that one designer can create a layout, then hand the project to another (usually junior) designer for layout implementation. The master pages here show that instructions are built into the master pages, such as "Use 'page head' style." A junior designer would be able to take the master pages, insert the specific product elements on each page, apply the predefined style sheets, and finish the catalog in a reasonable amount of time.

Si meliora dies, ut vina, poemata reddit, scire velim, chartis pretium quotus arroget annus. scriptor abhinc annos centum qui decidit, inter perfectos veteresque referri debet an inter vilis atque novos? Excludat iurgia finis, "Est vetus atque probus, centum qui perficit annos." Quid, qui deperiit minor uno mense velanno, inter quos referendus erit? an quos et praesens et postera respuat aetas? "Iste quidem veteres inter ponetur honeste, qui vel mense brevi vel toto est iunior anno." Utor permisso, caudaeque pilos ut equinae paulatim vello unum, demo etiam unum, dum cadat elusus ratione ruentis acervi, qui redit in fastos et virtutem aestimat annis miraturque nihil nisi quod Libitina sacravit.

An example of greeked type.

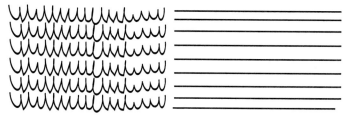

Ws and rules can show where text will be placed in a layout.

don't have greeking capability, other designers type a non-sequitur statement like "Body text goes here" and duplicate the sentence until they have 800 words.

If you are not using a software program to plan your layout, you still have a number of options. You might cut a block of copy from a magazine to show where text will eventually be placed. Another option is to simply pencil in Ws or rules to show text placement. (Note: this may be a better idea, since actual-but-incorrect type in a sample layout can confuse clients.)

Creating Visual Interest

Because the grid or master page is a structured formatting tool, it is easy for page design to look imprisoned by the grid. Several concepts allow you to create imaginative layouts while still using a grid: the "Z," the focal point, rhythm, contrast, and unity.

COLUMNS

If you decide to use more than one column of type in a publication, column width is generally governed by the size of the font you use. Column width is typically determined by the length of 1.5 complete alphabets in that typeface at the point size you will be using in the final document.

1.5 alphabets determine a standard column width for this typeface:

abcdefghijklmnopqrstuvwxyzabcdefghijklm

Keep in mind that shorter column widths are easier to read for most people (except for very short lines, which can appear choppy and cluttered with hyphenated words). As a general rule, the more literate your target audience is, the longer your columns can be. More experienced readers, compared to average readers, have less difficulty tracking down to the next line. Margins should be at least twice as wide as the gutter, or the space between columns.

Journal of Latin Study

Si meliora dies, ut vina poemata reddit, scire velim, chartis

Si meliora dies, ut vina, poemata reddit, scire velim, chartis pretium quotus arroget annus. scriptor abhinc annos centum qui decidit, inter perfectos veteresque referri debet an inter vilis atque novos? Excludat iurgia finis. "Est vetus atque probus, centum qui perficit annos." Quid, qui deperiit minor uno mense velamo, inter quos referendus erit? an quos et praesens et postera respuat aetas? "Iste quidem veteres inter ponetur honeste, qui vel mense brevi vel toto est iunior anno." Uter permisso, caudaeque pilos ut equinae paulatim vello unum, demo etiam unum, dum cadat elusus ratione ruentis acervi, qui redit in fastos et virtutem aestimat annis miraturque nihil nisi quod Libitina sacravit.

Si meliora dies, ut vina, poemata reddit, scire velim, chartis pretium quotus arroget annus. scriptor abhinc annos centum qui decidit, inter perfectos veteresque referri debet an inter vilis atque novos? Excludat iurgia finis. "Est vetus atque probus, centum qui perficit annos." Quid, qui deperiit minor uno mense velamo, inter quos referendus erit? an quos et praesens et postera respuat aetas? "Iste quidem veteres inter ponetur honeste, qui vel mense brevi vel toto est iunior anno." Uter permisso, caudaeque pilos ut equinae paulatim vello unum, demo etiam unum, dum cadat elusus ratione ruentis acervi, qui redit in fastos et virtutem aestimat annis miraturque nihil nisi quod Libitina sacravit. "Est vetus atque probus, centum qui perficit annos." Quid, qui deperiit minor uno mense velamo, inter quos referendus erit? an quos et praesens et postera respuat aetas? "Iste qui-

dem veteres inter ponetur honeste, qui vel mense brevi vel toto est iunior anno." Uter permisso, caudaeque pilos ut equinae paulatim vello unum, demo etiam unum, dum cadat elusus ratione ruentis acervi, qui redit in fastos et virtutem aestimat annis miraturque

Nihil nisi quod Libitina sacravit. Si meliora dies, ut vina, poemata reddit, scire velim, chartis pretium quotus arroget annus. scriptor abhinc annos centum qui decidit, inter perfectos veteresque referri debet an inter vilis atque novos? Excludat iurgia finis. "Est vetus atque probus, centum qui perficit minor uno mense velamo, inter quos et praesens et postera respuat aetas? "Iste qui dem veteres inter ponetur honeste, qui vel mense brevi vel toto est iunior anno." Uter permisso, caudaeque pilos ut equinae paulatim vello unum, demo etiam unum, dum cadat elusus ratione ruentis acervi, qui redit in fastos et virtutem aestimat annis miraturque nihil nisi quod Libitina sacravit.

"Est vetus atque probus, centum qui perficit annos." Quid, qui deperiit minor uno mense velamo, inter quos referendus erit? an quos et praesens et postera respuat aetas? "Iste quidem veteres inter ponetur honeste, qui vel mense brevi vel toto est iunior anno." Uter permisso, caudaeque pilos ut equinae paulatim vello unum, demo etiam unum. Si meliora dies, ut vina, poemata reddit, scire velim, chartis pretium quotus arroget annus. scriptor abhinc annos centum qui decidit, inter perfectos veteresque referri debet an inter vilis atque novos? Excludat iurgia finis. "Est vetus atque probus, centum qui perficit annos." Quid, qui deperiit minor uno mense velamo, inter quos referendus erit? an quos et praesens et postera respuat aetas? "Iste qui-

Car Wax:
10 Tips from the Pros

Si meliora dies, ut vina, poemata reddit, scire velim, chartis pretium quotus arroget annus. scriptor abhinc annos centum qui decidit, inter perfectos veteresque referri debet an inter vilis atque novos? Excludat iurgia finis. "Est vetus atque probus, centum qui perficit annos." Quid, qui deperiit minor uno mense velamo, inter quos referendus erit? an quos et praesens et postera respuat aetas? "Iste quidem veteres inter ponetur honeste, qui vel mense brevi vel toto est iunior anno." Uter permisso, caudaeque pilos ut equinae paulatim vello unum, demo etiam unum, dum cadat elusus ratione ruentis acervi, qui redit in fastos et virtutem aestimat annis miraturque nihil nisi quod Libitina sacravit.

Si meliora dies, ut vina, poemata reddit, scire velim, chartis pretium quotus arroget annus. scriptor abhinc annos centum qui decidit, inter perfectos veteresque referri debet an inter vilis atque novos? Excludat iurgia finis. "Est vetus atque probus, centum qui perficit minor uno mense velamo, inter quos et praesens et postera respuat aetas? "Iste quidem veteres inter ponetur honeste, qui vel mense brevi vel toto est iunior anno." Uter permisso, caudaeque pilos ut equinae paulatim vello unum, demo etiam unum, dum cadat elusus ratione ruentis acervi, qui redit in fastos et virtutem aestimat annis miraturque nihil nisi quod Libitina sacravit.

Si meliora dies, ut vina, poemata reddit, scire velim, chartis pretium quotus arroget annus. scriptor abhinc annos centum qui decidit, inter perfectos veteresque referri debet an inter vilis atque novos? Excludat iurgia finis. "Est vetus atque probus, centum qui perficit annos." Quid, qui deperiit minor uno mense velamo, inter quos referendus erit? an quos et praesens et postera respuat aetas? "Iste quidem veteres inter ponetur honeste, qui vel mense brevi

vel toto est iunior anno." Uter permisso, caudaeque pilos ut equinae paulatim vello unum, demo etiam unum, dum cadat elusus ratione ruentis acervi, qui redit in fastos et virtutem aestimat annis miraturque nihil nisi quod Libitina sacravit.

Si meliora dies, ut vina, poemata reddit, scire velim, chartis pretium quotus arroget annus. scriptor abhinc annos centum qui decidit, inter perfectos veteresque referri debet an inter vilis atque novos? "Iste quidem veteres inter ponetur honeste, qui vel mense brevi vel toto est iunior anno." Uter permisso, caudaeque pilos ut equinae paulatim vello unum, demo etiam unum, dum cadat elusus ratione ruentis acervi, qui redit in fastos et virtutem aestimat annis miratur

Nihil nisi quod Libitina sacravit. Si meliora dies, ut vina, poemata reddit, scire velim, chartis pretium quotus arroget annus. scriptor abhinc annos centum qui decidit, inter perfectos vet-eresque referri debet an inter vilis atque novos? Excludat

iurgia finis. "Est vetus atque probus, centum qui perficit annos." Quid, qui deperiit minor uno mense velamo, inter quos referendus erit? an quos et praesens et postera respuat aetas? "Iste quidem veteres inter ponetur honeste, qui vel mense brevi vel toto est iunior anno." Uter permisso, caudaeque pilos ut equinae paulatim vello unum, demo etiam unum, dum cadat elusus ratione ruentis acervi, qui redit in fastos et virtutem aestimat annis miratur

"Est vetus atque probus, centum qui perficit annos." Quid, qui deperiit minor uno mense velamo, inter quos referendus erit? an quos et praesens et postera respuat aetas? "Iste quidem veteres inter ponetur honeste, qui vel mense brevi vel toto est iunior anno." Uter permisso, caudaeque pilos ut equinae pau-latim vello unum, demo etiam unum, dum cadat elusus ratione ruentis acervi, qui redit in fastos et virtutem aestimat annis miraturque nihil nisi quod Libitina sacravit. Uter permisso, caudaeque pilos ut equinae pau-latim vello unum. Si meliora dies, ut vina, poemata reddit, scire velim, chartis pretium quotus. Quid, qui deperiit minor uno mense velam-

Examples of appropriate column widths based on target market.

THE "Z"

People generally move across a printed page in a predictable way. The eye starts (at least in the Western world) at the upper-left corner, travels directly across to the top-right corner, moves diagonally to the lower-left corner, then moves across again to finish at the lower-right corner. (Note: It is a good idea to have some heavy element at the bottom right of the layout to stop the viewer's eye.)

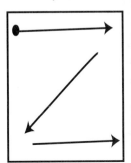

May 19 - 21, 2002
Miami Fishing Pier
Admission: $5.00
Seafood, WaterSports, Treasure Hunt, FUN!

The classic Z pattern.

THE FOCAL POINT OF THE PAGE

There is a certain, specific point on any page that people look at first. As mentioned several times previously, you don't need to know the psychological motivation behind this behavior, only that it exists. You can use this to your advantage when planning a page layout.

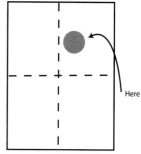

The "secret spot" for visual interest.

RHYTHM

Just like rhythm in music, visual *rhythm* helps to set the tone, pace, and progression through the piece from start to finish. A good marching piece helps melt away the miles with its brisk, repetitive cadence. A lilting waltz twirls you gracefully through the song. Samba music has a decidedly different way in which it sets the pace. The same concept can be applied to visual rhythm. By changing the shape, size, and value of the elements in a layout, you can lead the viewer through at an even tempo, or create variety. The rhythm sets the mood of the piece, and reinforces the overall tone. The simple example to the left illustrates this concept.

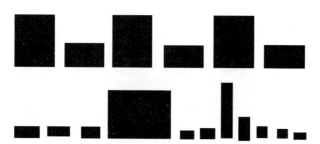

Visualize the rhythm created by these arrangements.

Some other important considerations for visual rhythm:

- People look at larger elements first.
- Larger elements are considered to have "slower" rhythm.
- Smaller elements are considered to have "faster" rhythm.
- People look at darker elements before lighter ones.
- People look at unusual shapes before conventional ones.

UNITY

Unifying a piece requires more than simply using the same type throughout, and more than using appropriate balance for the type of image conveyed. *Unity* refers to the overall compositional harmony of the elements. It is the sum-total of the proper

Notice:
Bank Foreclosure

Party!!

Appropriate use of page proportion and balance.

weight of type, negative and positive space, balance, rhythm, and tone. Following is a simple checklist for compositional unity:

- Is the page proportion appropriate to the message?

- Is the balance appropriate to the message?

- Is the type choice appropriate to the message?

- Do the typefaces all work together?

- Are rules and borders (weight and style) harmonious with the type choices?

- Are the shapes created by pictures and borders harmonious?

- Is there a consistency of style? Or does it look like three different designers had input?

Layout Makeovers

The first line of the body copy for this article is, "Got your attention?" The answer is "Not likely." Of course, the headline might work — even though it looks like one very long headline instead of a headline and a subheadline. But once readers move to the extremely long, seemingly endless block of text, they are not likely to read past the first two lines. The rather amateur page ends with a reverse-type, centered footer with the newsletter name.

The example on the right breaks the "sea-of-text" syndrome into three columns to improve readability. Since there are no graphic elements to accompany the article, a quote within the piece (a headline from the National Enquirer) is highlighted in a different and larger font. The page is further broken down by adding a different box which includes two graphic elements; the original story is continued on the following page of the newsletters. There is no rule that an entire article must appear on the same page. In this case — a long, unillustrated article — breaking up the text can keep the reader's visual interest and can make a rather small-budget project look more professional.

You might also consider a variation from the standard horizontal title bar of a newsletter. The newsletter on the bottom is a complete redesign, including a new title that reflects the publisher's intention and attitude. The vertical title bar adds a graphic element to an otherwise boring front page; the newsletter is printed with only black ink, so the options for variation are limited. The subheadline is in a different font with a leading line, which breaks up the long block of text more than the same font subheadline used in the left version. The newsletter uses the same bold, heavy style throughout.

As a beginning designer, this chapter provided you with the basics of layout design. The rules mentioned previously will provide a solid foundation for any design project. They are, in fact, so important that we list them again:

- Is the page proportion appropriate to the message?

- Is the balance appropriate to the message?

- Is the type choice appropriate to the message?

- Do the typefaces all work together?

- Are rules and borders (weight and style) harmonious with the type choices?

- Are the shapes created by pictures and borders harmonious?

- Is there a consistency of style? Or does it look like three different designers had input?

CHAPTER 7

Line

*What concerns me is not the way things are,
rather the way people think they are.*

—EPICETUS (ROMAN PHILOSOPHER)

The word *line* has several different meanings in graphic design. The standard definition, of course, is "a series of points that is longer than it is wide and is different than the background in terms of color or value." This is true, but line is much than that.

Lines From a Designer's Viewpoint

Designers use lines for many things—to define the edge or shape of a two-dimensional object, to sketch out spatial relationships, to sketch thumbnails before creating a layout, to illustrate or reinforce explanations, or to represent three-dimensional objects. The mind uses visual shorthand to interpret these lines. Use of line can be divided into two broad categories, the physical characteristics of a line and the content of a line.

LINES AS OBJECTS: PHYSICAL CHARACTERISTICS OF LINES

Designers use lines, in their simplest form, to divide space. Lines denote a boundary; for example, they can be used to divide the writing area of a letterhead from the area reserved for the company logotype and information.

Lines can also be used to form texture or to create decoration. The weight or thickness of the line has a direct bearing on the effectiveness of the illusion created.

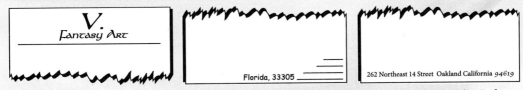

Example of (left) line used to divide space; (middle) line used to create textural interest; and (right) "line" of type.

The word "line" is also used to describe a column width of type. If you squint your eyes, the individual letters in a line of type become a blurry long mark on the page. The weight of this "line" becomes a compositional element in and of itself.

by A.M. Giraldo

Example of line used for direction. The scroll of musical notes returns the eye back to the name of the event

LINE DIRECTION, IMPLICATION, AND EMOTION

Line can be used to direct the viewer's eye around a page. People have a tendency to follow the visual path of a line; keep this in mind whenever you want to direct your viewer's attention.

Also keep in mind that (in Western cultures) people read a page left to right, top to bottom. If the visual information doesn't follow this preconceived notion of visual information structure, the viewer has little patience and quickly loses interest. The viewer will move on, rather than spend time deconstructing the information.

One of the best features of lines is that they don't have to even be there to be effective. People mentally create lines where there are none, imposing structure based on the slightest suggestion of a visual path. This tendency is covered in the Gestalt Theory of Visual Organization, and has been written about extensively. You don't need to know the deeper psychological details. As a designer you only need to know that this phenomena exists (known as the use of *implied line*), and how to take advantage of it.

People also tend to "connect the dots" to form a path, shape, or even a whole image if the dots are regularly spaced and not too far apart. Designers can use this subtle and effective technique to their advantage, using implied lines to direct the viewer's attention throughout a layout instead of relying on real lines.

Example of implied line. We construct a visual path connecting the elements of a set. How far apart do the elements have to be before we no longer see them as a unit?

A real-world example of implied line is demonstrated by Ana Maria Giraldo. Her project illustrates the issue of elderly abandonment. Her thumbnails and final visual solution follow.

The sketch on the upper left shows good foreground/background relationship, but is square, formal, and lacks drama. The upper-right illustration is more dynamic in the arrangement of elements, but lacks visual subtlety. The family portrait on the bottom left is too simple. The final sketch uses the side view of the seated figure (from the first illustration) with a better, more visually sophisticated grouping of the family — the perfect representation of elderly abandonment. The illustration relies heavily on the implied line between the child and seated grandparent to create visual and emotional tension.

The thumbnails. Can you see why the final thumbnail is the most powerful?

Notice the visual tension created by the gap between the child's hand and the back of the wheelchair.

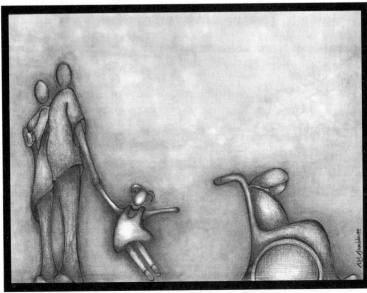

The Emotional Content of a Line

The emotional content of a line is the emotional response that we associate with linear movement. We tend to think of diagonal lines as energetic and active; horizontal, heavy lines are considered stable and static. Several emotional responses seem to be universal:

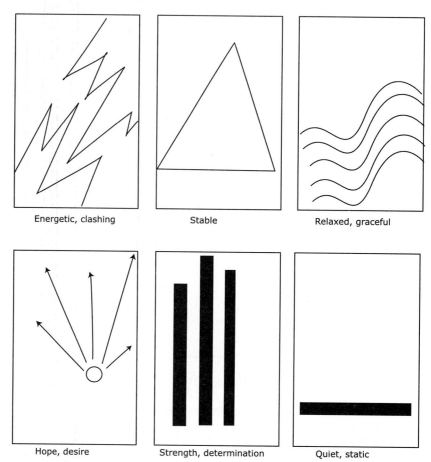

Energetic, clashing	Stable	Relaxed, graceful
Hope, desire	Strength, determination	Quiet, static

Look through magazines, old calendars, greeting cards, or posters to find lines which illustrate different emotions:

- Energetic, thrusting lines
- Placid, calm lines
- Tension lines
- Lazy lines
- Radiating lines

What conveys the specific emotion in each image? Become familiar with the way different kinds of line can be used to manipulate the viewer.

CHAPTER 8

Type

Typography, like architecture, can take many forms and be either sublime or ridiculous. Like architecture, typography can be responsible or irresponsible, boring or exciting.

—MASSINO VIGNELLI, *TYPOGRAPHY 2*

Type is one of the most effective means to establish the mood or theme of a design project. The title, headline, and body copy, as well as how they relate to each other, establish an ambience, attitude, or mood.

Since the mid 1980s, the word "font" has been used interchangeably with the word "type." A font is described as all the characters that make up a specific type style, such as Aldus Roman. "Type," on the other hand, is a generic word referring to letter form in general.

Type is divided into categories, the broadest, most general groups organized by the letterform. Type categories are further refined into classes—or classifications—which share specific features, such as thick-and-thin strokes. These are further broken down into families, or type styles sharing a common design. Families are divided into specific faces, such as regular, italic, bold, extended, or condensed.

Type Categories

The five primary categories of type are serif, sans serif, script, decorative, and pi.

SERIF TYPE

The stroke at the top or base of letters, or the ear or spur on some letters, are elements that help you identify serif type. Because of their formal, traditional appearance, serif fonts are also commonly used to convey a conservative, dignified image. Except for Bodoni, these typefaces are easy to read and are used extensively for long passages of text. Bodoni has strong thick and thin strokes, a low x-height, and long ascenders and descenders, making it a less desirable choice for text-heavy documents.

Times
Garamond
Bodoni

Serif fonts are characterized by strokes at the top and base of the letters.

Arial
Helvetica
Futura

Sans-serif fonts have no stroke at the top or base.

Boulevard
Brush Script
Vivaldi

Script fonts appear to be created with a brush or pen.

CASH
Paintbrush
Papyrus

Decorative fonts usually look like the name of the font.

Σψμβολ

Pi fonts are used to set special characters or symbols.

SANS-SERIF TYPE

In French, sans means "without;" hence, sans serif means "without the stroke." Sans-serif fonts have no stroke at the top or base. Because of the legibility of these type-faces, they are a good choice for labelling illustrations. Because many newspaper headlines are set in a sans-serif typeface, we have come to associate "the facts" with sans-serif fonts. When reversing type out of a background, a sans-serif face is a good choice.

SCRIPT (INVITATION) TYPE

Any typeface that has the appearance of being created with a pen or a brush, whether the letters are connected or unconnected, is a script typeface. They are often used for invitations or announcements, and sometime for logos. Use script fonts with caution; they are not well-received in some schools of design thought, and are in-appropriate for certain target audiences. Script type is easy to distinguish; it often has the word "script" in its name.

DECORATIVE TYPE

Decorative, or display typefaces, are meant to be used in headlines, and to convey specific meaning. You can likely guess what the fonts Valhalla, Eyechart, and Quetzalcoatl look like even without seeing the letters. Keep in mind that decorative fonts can be extremely elaborate. The primary consideration for type should always be read-ability; it is never a good idea to introduce a complex type style into the body of a document.

PI (SYMBOL) TYPE

Pi fonts, often called symbol, logo, or ornaments, are used to insert symbols into text that are re-used many times. A pi font is a collection of related symbols. These might include characters in a math font, a company logo, blocks in a crossword puzzle, borders for a page, credit cards, astrologic symbols, or map symbols. If there is a need, the font is often created. This saves much time and space in documents, where a logo may even be used as a bullet point. There are hundreds of pi fonts.

Type Families

A type family is a set of fonts that share a common letterform construction. The fonts within a family are closely related, using variations of the basic letterform. A font designer will create a master font, then consistently alter one feature, such as character width, or weight, to create another font within the same family. Some common variations are extended, condensed, outline, bold, and thin; regardless of the treatment, the original font is still recognizable.

UNIVERSE ROMAN
UNIVERSE ULTRA CONDENSED
UNIVERSE CONDENSED
UNIVERSE EXTENDED

A master is altered to create different fonts within the same family.

Desktop-publishing sofware generally allows you to imitate the condensing and expanding of type—badly. If you would like the condensed version of a font, but none exists, you can alter the vertical and horizontal dimensions of any font to either reduce or enlarge that dimension. Be careful, though; scaling a font will distort the design of the letterform.

Normal
70% horizontal scale
90% horizontal scale
110% horizontal scale

These four lines are the same font at the same point size. We assigned different values to the horizontal scale. Note how the relationship between thick and thin strokes is affected.

A type style is a treatment that can be applied to any font: italic, bold, outline, and so on. This kind of style is generally applied in word processing or desktop-publishing software. Type styles are used to add variety or emphasis within a body of text. Do not randomly italicize or embolden text; follow the rules that have been developed over time, or have some valid reason for using styles. Don't apply bold to a word just because a paragraph is entirely set in regular type.

Certain styles are dictated by convention; titles of movies, books, magazines, or any other published work are set in italics; foreign words are also commonly set in italics. The *Chicago Manual of Style*, *Associated Press Stylebook and Libel Manual*, and similar guides discuss at length the appropriate use of italics.

When you are designing for print, you must properly assign italics and bold, or you may be surprised when the job is imaged. If you select Bold or Italic from the menu, and no bold or italic versions exist for that font, what you styled will print in the regular style or that type may default to Courier. Another trap lies in what happens when you click on Bold. If, for example, you are working in the Minion typeface and click on Bold, you will get Minion Semibold. If you are working in ITC Garamond Book and click on Bold, you will get ITC Garamond Book. It is always safest to choose your font from the type menu.

Kerning, Tracking, and Leading

There's more to using type well than just choosing a family of type to use. How that type looks on the page is dependent, to a great extent, upon the tightness and looseness of letters, and the amount of space allowed between lines. While they are generically know as letterspace and linespace, we will address the elements of spacing: kerning, tracking, and leading.

Kerning refers to the space between any two letters. Letters within a font have assigned character widths; typewriter fonts, and fonts designed to imitate the look of a typewriter have uniform character widths, meaning that every letter in the alphabet takes the same horizontal space, while other fonts have varying letter width.

DOW
DOW

When the space between the O and W is decreased (bottom), the bounding boxes actually overlap, but the space between the characters becomes more pleasing.

Word-processing and desktop-publishing software use the font's default kerning pairs, which are adequate for most projects. Inexpensive fonts often have few or no kerning pairs built into them, whereas most professionally-designed fonts have hundreds or even thousands of built-in kerning pairs.

Some letter combinations, especially in large sizes, can look awkward without additional kerning. Consider a letterform as a rectangle; the space that tightly surrounds the character is called the bounding box. If you place a "D" next to an "O" followed by a "W," you will see that the combination of letters looks either too crowded or too far apart:

Tracking, unlike kerning, adjusts the letterspace for a range of letters, not simply the space between two letters. If you use type justified to both margins, you may notice that different lines throughout the text have different spacing between the letters. Desktop-publishing programs can be programmed to do a decent job of dividing the space (called *hyphenation and justification*, or H&J), but they are not perfect.

Tracking is an excellent way to get rid of widows and orphans at the end of a paragraph. Use caution though; too much tracking can make the type appear crowded, making it virtually unreadable.

This is a bad example of tracking. Too much space has been removed from between the letters.

This is also a bad example of tracking. There is too much space between each letter, which makes the type lose meaning.

Leading (led•ding) is the space between lines of text measured from baseline to baseline. Line spacing should be sufficient so that letters do not crash into one another, allowing for the depth of descenders and the height of ascenders. In general, headlines and smaller blocks of text have proportionally less leading than do large blocks of text. Most desktop publishing programs assign as the default leading 120% of the letter size, so type set in 12 point type is assigned 14.4 points of leading.

Leading

Baseline to baseline

Leading

As a general rule, spacing between lines should make reading comfortable for the reader. If you put too much space between lines, the text block no longer holds together as an element. Lines spaced too tightly can appear crowded and confusing. Leading depends on the words in the text block; a line with no descenders can be more tightly spaced than one with many letters falling below the baseline.

Type Do's and Don'ts

DO:
- Use serif type to convey an attitude of traditional, conventional values and stability.
- Use sans-serif type to label illustrations.
- Use sans-serif type for a modern look, or for a book for children.
- Use decorative type for a "novelty" treatment.
- Use decorative type sparingly.
- Use decorative type in display sizes only (24 point or larger).
- Use script type for announcements and invitations.
- Use type appropriate to your message

Requiem Mass
Requiem Mass

Your type choices should be appropriate to the message of your design. The rounded, sans-serif font (top) does not convey the solemnity of the occasion.

The top example uses four different fonts with no apparent rationale for style choice and layout. Script typefaces are commonly used to portray elegance; in this instance, though, the script is incongruous with the rest of the ad and suggests "amateur" more than "elegant."

Each element in the ad is a different size; the viewer has no idea which element to look at first, and which are the most important elements. Based on font size, the owners' names are more important than the body copy. The layout and arrangement give little help, since the heavy, bold bottom line is as large as the headline. The headline, address, and owners' names are strictly centered, while the company logo and copy block are off center and unbalanced. Italics are generally used to highlight important text; in this instance, the entire copy block is italicized, which negates that emphasis.

The middle example eliminates the script typeface entirely, since it adds no value to the piece. The headline stands out more as a reverse block. The body copy is clearly the second element, with more white space on the top and bottom; italics are not necessary, and have been removed.

Though much better than the first, the second example is still problematic. The owners' names are the same size as the headline; if the viewer simply follows top-to-bottom convention, the ad might work. But at a quick glance, the viewer is not certain where to look first.

The bottom example uses much smaller type for the owners' names. The reversed headline uses the largest type, and is now clearly the most important element. The body copy uses the next largest type size, and so on down the page. Right alignment also helps to move the viewer's eye from top to bottom.

Helping Develop
Wilton Manor's Future

Nathan
Real Estate

We provide complete real estate services for the Wilton Manor area. Whether you're buying, selling or listing commercial property, give us a call.

201 East Blvd. Wilton Manors FL 33305

Dave Nathan, Jake and Sophie Nathan

Helping Develop Wilton Manor's Future

We provide complete real estate services for Wilton Manors. Whether you're buying, selling or listing commercial property, give us a call.

Nathan Real Estate

201 East Blvd. Wilton Manors, FL 33305

Dave Nathan, Jake and Sophie Nathan

Helping Develop Wilton Manor's Future

We provide complete real estate services for Wilton Manors. Whether you're buying, selling or listing commercial property, give us a call.

Nathan
Real Estate
201 East Blvd. Wilton Manors, FL 33305

Dave Nathan, Jake and Sophie Nathan

It is most important that you *do* use members of a family of fonts, in different sizes and styles throughout a publication rather than using several different kinds of type. You gain a much more professional look with a variety of weights and point sizes. The hallmark of a well-designed piece is the controlled, careful use of type.

DON'T:
- Use type in all upper case. It is harder to read than upper and lowercase letters.
- Use several different typefaces within a project. Stick to a couple of different fonts.
- Use unkerned type for display purposes.
- Leave too much or too little space between lines of type.

If you wonder whether or not you should use a special effect with type, try it. If you're still in doubt, don't.

Using Type to Create a Mood or Idea

by M. Upadhya

Type can create an attitude, set a mood, or establish a theme. A "spring" catalog might use decorative or display type with soft curvy lines, airy spacing, and wafting ascenders and descenders. The next time you have a design problem, brainstorm ideas that use a specific text treatment. For instance, what type treatment would convey the idea of spring?

Notice the airy letters and tendril-like strokes in this solution to the "spring" problem. The open vine shapes that make up the letter "L" are carried into the weight of the letters in the rest of the word, creating a link between the decorative, hand-drawn "L" and the letters.

Logo and corporate identity design provide an excellent opportunity to examine the appropriate use of type. Compare these logo concepts:

by Andy Bing

You can clearly (top left) see that a sans-serif font will not work for "OATS." The second example (top middle) switches to a serif font, but it does not provide any visual link to the company's identity. The third example (top right) uses a heavier serif font and looks much better, though there is still no visual significance of this type choice. The final solution (left) shows a much more appropriate type choice. The stencil-like type is reminiscent of the lettering on an old burlap oat bag, giving the specific type choice both visual and contextual meaning.

The same concept should be applied to any design project for which you need to select type.

plans and your goals and you will go beyond where every-one else has gone before. You will achieve more than most people ever, ever get to in their life. You will be a winner.

your boots attached to their bindings. Or maybe it's just putting on an old T-shirt, turning off the ringers on the phone, drinking a beer and putting your feet up on the coffee table for a week.

Use this big question as positive motivation to get you to this very spot. How can you put your business on the fast track to make enough extra cash to go? How can you put your business on auto pilot so you can take the time off? Use the action planning sheet in this issue to help you develop the plan that will get you to that delightful vacation paradise.

Happy visualization.

Printers' Marketing Newsletter   6

plans and your goals and you will go beyond where every-one else has gone before. You will achieve more than most people ever, ever get to in their life. You will be a winner.

your boots attached to their bindings. Or maybe it's just putting on an old T-shirt, turning off the ringers on the phone, drinking a beer and putting your feet up on the coffee table for a week.

Use this big question as positive motivation to get you to this very spot. How can you put your business on the fast track to make enough extra cash to go? How can you put your business on auto pilot so you can take the time off? Use the action planning sheet in this issue to help you develop the plan that will get you to that delightful vacation paradise.

Happy visualization.

Explosive Marketing Strategies 6

The top example shows the old footer that was placed on each page of a newsletter. The plain black box with sans-serif, reverse type includes all of the relevant information — newsletter title and page number. But what does the sans-serif font convey about the information?

The bottom example takes the rather boring footer and recreates it visually. The type is a handwritten script, suggesting the way a fuse would coil; it is also distorted to look like the ashes that would be left from a burning fuse; the dynamite provides a placeholder for the page number. All of the vital information is still present, but the visual presentation is far more interesting than the plain black box and sans-serif font.

The following illustrations show one artist's solution for illustrating the concept "push."

Very rough thumbnails.

Rough for the chosen visual solution.

This second-step rough allows further modifications to the size, placement, and letterform weight. Once the sketch is drawn at larger size, it becomes obvious that the letter "P" needs more slant to push the rest of the word acutely. You can now see that the rest of the word also needs to be much more crowded. Finally, it might help the message if the word container was a bit cramped, as if the word were being "pushed" into a tight space.

by M. Germano

Final "push" solution.

The following illustrations show a few more examples of using type to illustrate a concept. You might design letters in your display text to reflect a theme or meaning.

by Christopher Feehan

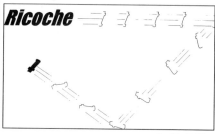

by M. Phillips

by S. Friedfeld

The solution for "Home Work" uses a bold sans-serif font and typical tools found around the house to lend a work-type of character to the words:

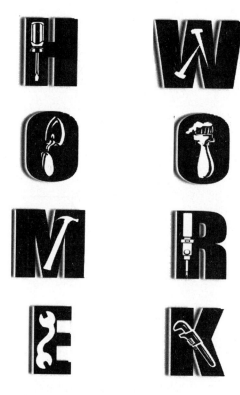

You might also use imagery associated with the intended message to create a typeface, as in the Witchy typeface:

Thumbnails to generate the Witchy typeface by A. M. Giraldo

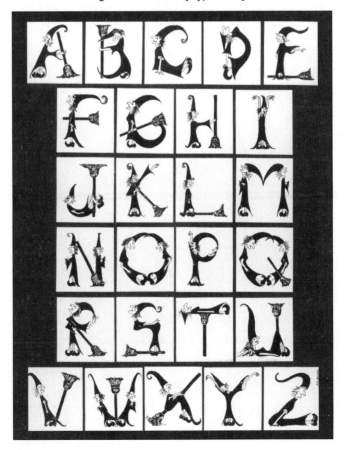

CHAPTER 9

Color

The purest and most thoughtful minds are those which love color the most

— JOHN RUSKIN

There is an extensive collection of writing available on color perception, color theory, and color reproduction. It is not our purpose here to go into great depth about the many aspects of color. Nor do we intend to tell you what colors to use in your design work. Rather, this chapter intends to give you a very general overview of color, specifically those issues that you should be aware of as a designer.

Color Perception and Meaning

Recall the chapter on symbolism. Color has both cultural and psychological significance. Consider clothing — how many different conventions dictate clothing color (in Western culture)? White for weddings, black for funerals. Don't wear white after Labor Day. Red or blue suggest political affiliation, loyalty and patriotism, or might be a symbol of gang activity. Wear pastels in the spring, jewel tones in the fall. The list goes on. These conventions carry over beyond clothing, and affect your creative flow.

Think of what each of these "colored" phrases refer to:
Green-eyed monster
White wedding
Blue-blooded

From another perspective, what colors come to mind?
Warmth
Danger
Fear

Of course this doesn't mean that green only suggests jealousy, or white always symbolizes purity. Two issues to keep in mind when working with color:

- Try to avoid the cliche.
- Color doesn't always have to be symbolic.

Rather than thinking of color symbolism as a limitation, use it to your advantage. Think of what you are trying to say with your design; brainstorm what colors might effectively convey that message.

Also consider what colors might be inappropriate for your design, and list the reasons why. Once this list is complete, re-examine the reasons. You may be able to use the opposite of what might be expected to make your point for you. Of course, people typically use pastel colors in the spring and jewel tones in the fall. But don't bind yourself with convention, especially when selecting colors.

MEMORY COLOR

Many things in our world are specific colors. Police cars are white, fire trucks are red; the sky is blue, grass is green; traffic lights are red, yellow, and green. People inherently know what color something is, even if it's printed in black-and-white.

Color can be a very effective branding tool, as important as layout for many companies. If you see a Coca-Cola can on a black-and-white television, you still know what color it is, right? On a similar note, if you see the red can with white swirl, even when the words aren't visible, you still know what is in the can. Color is so important to Coca-Cola that the company holds a copyright on that particular red ink.

Perhaps more importantly from a designer's viewpoint, people know what color something should be. You might use this to your advantage—wouldn't you stop and take notice of a park with purple grass? People are drawn to anything that strays from their expectations.

You can likely guess what color these foods are supposed to be. But what if the broccoli was blue, or the tomatoes were purple? The unexpected can be an effective design tool.

COMPLEMENTARY COLORS

The image to the right shows a very simplified model of the color wheel. *Complementary color* means opposite colors on the color wheel. Complementary background colors in your design can enhance and strengthen the appearance of what you are trying to highlight, which is especially useful for point-of-purchase and packaging design. Red apples are displayed in green or blue casing, and bags of carrots frequently have blue or purple lettering. The complementary colors make the produce look brighter, which leads people to think it is fresher.

(Color wheel labels: Orange, Red, Yellow, Magenta, Green, Violet, Cyan, Blue)

Using the Proper Color Mode

Whether a piece of art is created digitally or by using traditional media, there are two types of color that may be used when the art is printed: *process* (CMYK) *color* and *spot color*. In today's digital age, it benefits an artist to have at least a rudimentary understanding of what happens when a job is printed.

Although today's requirements often include preparing files for use on the Internet, those rules are much simpler to understand because the display you're working on is essentially the same as someone else's. (See Chapter 17, Web Design and Multimedia, for more information about using color when designing Web sites.) When it comes to putting ink on paper, the number and complexity of the variables increase geometrically.

When you begin planning a design, you need to consider what the design will eventually be used for. If you're planning concepts for a logo, how will that logo be used? Logos and corporate identity have very important reproduction requirements. Whatever you create will likely be on everything the company has — letterhead, business cards, advertising, newsletters, annual reports, and Web sites. The logo that you create for a company has to work for all of these end uses. It has to look equally good on a black-and-white newsletter, a full-color magazine ad, a two-color letterhead, and the company Web site.

PRINTING PROCESSES

Fine art media (oil paint, pastels, pencils) can produce a greater range or *color gamut* than traditional printing processes. But keep in mind that fine art is not usually created for reproduction. Graphic design, however, begins with the idea that whatever you design will be reproduced in quantity.

Do you remember the primary colors from elementary school? Red, yellow, blue. Mix your red and yellow crayons, you get orange; blue and yellow crayons make green; red mixed with blue equals purple. This model is a very simplistic version of the printing process. Red, yellow, and blue are actually magenta, yellow, and cyan (how many six-year-olds know what cyan is?)

Traditional printing uses process colors of ink—cyan, magenta, yellow, and black—to re-create design. Theoretically, the three primary colors (CMY) combine to produce black. Realistically, though, pigment impurities usually result in a muddy, brownish gray; black ink (K) is added as a fourth color to allow cleaner blacks.

Color printing is actually an illusion. When you look at *Sports Illustrated, New Yorker, Smithsonian Magazine,* or your local color newspaper, you might think there is a complete range of colors in the images, but there isn't. Only the four colors of ink are used to simulate over 18,000 different colors—flesh tones, blue skies, green grasses, yellow bananas, or rich red velvet. But look closely and there are only four inks.

Different percentages of the four primaries are used to create printed colors, or *process builds.* It may be a good idea to have access to a *process color chart* when you're working; several are available commercially, or your printer may have one specifically produced to match their press.

Superblack. As mentioned previously, black ink is added to the three primaries to allow cleaner black printing. Instead of simply specifying K=100, many designers enhance black areas of design with percentages of the other primaries. If you add cyan to 100% black, the black areas of your design will have a cooler appearance; add magenta and your blacks will look warmer. These superblacks have greater ink density than simple black, and can greatly enhance your design work.

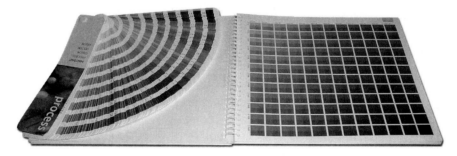

Two different options for specifying color.

SPOT COLOR

Printing does allow other options, if you are willing to pay for them. There are a number of *color systems* (Pantone and Trumatch are two examples) on the market that allow you to specify a color with a single ink (called spot or *PMS* color) instead of a process color build. Most of the systems sell chip books, similar to what you would see in a home-improvement paint department. You can select a color from these books and be assured that the color you pick is the one that is printed.

Spot colors are created by mixing inks together in a bucket at the printer —literally. Printers have a collection of colored inks, with names like Rubine Red, Reflex Blue, Violet, and Green. Spot colors are used for two primary purposes: adding a second color to a regular black print job (two-color printing), or adding a 5th color, such as that required for a corporate logo, to a four-color job. If you want to use a spot color, you must pick it from a Pantone or TruMatch book. You can't create custom spot colors because the printer won't know which inks to mix together to reproduce what you create on your monitor.

The benefit to using special ink systems is that you know what you are getting — closer to the way you would select an oil paint or colored pencil. The disadvantage, though, is that these specialty inks are expensive, and can make the production process very time-consuming. Most printing presses can print four, six, or possibly eight different ink colors at once. One book publisher hired a designer to lay out a 19-chapter book. The designer used a different spot color for each chapter's heading; other colors were also added for special sections of the book to produce a final document that specified no less then 34 colors. To print a book designed this way, every page would have to go through a four-color press nine times! The book had to be entirely redesigned.

Be careful when designing with specialty inks. Since the printing processes generally use process color, be aware that anything you designate as a specialty color may have to be converted to a process build. Most of the specialty systems provide conversion charts, so that you'll be able to come close to the same color. Desktop-publishing software may even be able to apply the conversion for you. Be aware, however, that special colors will *not* look the same when printed as process builds.

Specialty inks allow you to design with colors that do not exist in the process color gamut, such as fluorescent or translucent colors, or metallics. These types of colors cannot be produced using process printing, so specialty inks are the only option. Anything you design with one of these colors will always have to be printed with special inks; if the design needs to be printed on other documents (like a logo) or displayed on the Web, you will have to rework the design to remove the special colors.

Many designers combine speciality inks with process color printing. A six-color pressrun might combine CMYK with one specialty color and a varnish, or with two specialty colors. This can be especially useful if a company's logo was designed with a spot or special color.

Duotones. If your budget is small, but you don't want to use only black, consider printing with two colors. (You can add even more variation to your two-color design by selecting a colored paper.) Black-and-white photos can be printed as duotones, which print highlights and shadows as shades of gray while the midtones are printed in another color. You may also consider using two different colors instead of black and one color. If you choose this method, though, be aware that at least one of the colors should still be dark.

RGB COLOR

Color monitors have an even smaller range of possible colors. Monitors (and televisions) use red, green, and blue light to re-create the colors you see on a screen. Different monitors have different *color depth* (or *bit depth*), which means the number of colors that can be defined for each pixel on your screen. Monitors range from one-bit (the old black-and-white monitors) to 24- or 32-bit (which can display millions of colors). The more colors you want, the more processing power is required.

When you're preparing images for the Internet, this is the mode to work in. One of the most important considerations when coloring objects for the Web is that you use a palette that's "safe" when viewed on Windows, Macintosh, WebTV, Unix, or Linux computers. Use it whenever you're creating images that will be eventually used on the Internet or an interactive CD.

Monitor display capabilities are very important for Web design. No two monitors are alike, and many people do not have the processing power to view millions of colors. Current standards define a palette of 216 "Web-safe" colors that you can safely use in designing a Web site, and allow you to be fairly certain that what you see is the same thing other viewers will see. This palette is built into most Web design software.

COLOR MANAGEMENT

We've already discussed the color differences between traditional art media, the printing process, and monitors. Desktop publishing added a wealth of capability to the design process; it also, however, added a few extra problems.

Because color differs from printer to printer, you can expect the same color variation to occur between the different elements of your desktop system. You don't need to understand the mechanics involved in color management, other than to be aware that there are differences. If you scan a photo, view it on your monitor, and print it on your inkjet printer, you can practically guarantee that the three images will look very different. If you send that same scanned image to a commercial printer, you can assume that it will produce a fourth variation of the picture.

As you gain experience in desktop graphic design, you will be able to more precisely predict what a color will look like when it's finally printed.

COLOR VIEWING

When you specify a color for a design, consider how the final product will be used. Lighting conditions can strongly influence the appearance of a color. If a product is going to be used or seen in bright white light, your color choices are largely unlimited. However, certain types of light limit the range of color with which you should design. Stores frequently have a yellow light cast, which means that signage will not look the same as it did in your fluorescent-lit office when you designed it. Red light is used in many retail outlets, which will drastically alter the appearance of cooler colors. Color appearance under different lighting conditions does not necessarily have to be bad, but it is an issue you need to be aware of.

BLACK-AND-WHITE (OR GREEN-AND-WHITE...)

Would you even consider buying a television that only shows black-and-white? Probably not. But in the design world, black-and-white can be just as powerful as color. Black-and-white images don't need to look like they were produced on a copy machine. A more appropriate term to describe black-and-white design is *grayscale*, which uses shades of gray to reproduce photographic images with only one ink color.

When color television and printing became readily available, everyone started using splashy, brilliant, colorful design. Black-and-white design lost its appeal for a while and was considered "cheap" or "old-fashioned." But as all design trends go, black-and-white has regained acceptance in the design world. Everything from movies to television ads to magazines to fine art have re-embraced black-and-white. Lack of color can be just as (if not more) effective than full glossy color.

Black-and-white conveys a very specific message — classic, "retro" (interestingly this still means "old-fashioned," but now it's acceptable) and distinguished. Think of the products that use black-and-white television and magazine ads — perfume, jewelry, luxury cars. Companies like DeBeers and Mercedes use black-and-white in their television and print advertising to suggest sophistication. Black-and-white also suggests tradition — Mercedes has been around for a long time.

Of course black-and-white is not the best solution for every design problem. But if you are working with a limited budget, black-and-white can create effective solutions.

Suggestions for Using Color

Color is largely a matter of personal choice and preference. It is not our intention or place to tell you to use blue as a complementary color to orange. However, there are some things to consider when choosing the colors for your design:

- Does your design look like a rainbow exploded?
  Too much color can be as ineffective as no color; projects should have some identifiable color scheme to maintain unity.

- Does your design use complements to the main color scheme for highlighted items?

- Are your color choices appropriate to the intended audience?

- Do the colors work within your client's preferences or corporate identity?

- Would a bright, vibrant color scheme convey your message more effectively than a pastel? Or would the message work better in muted tones?

- Does your design work with four-color process, or would black-and-white or duotone printing be more effective?

CHAPTER 10

Paper, Binding, and Finishing

What we call the beginning is often the end and to make an end the beginning is to make a beginning. The end is where we start from.

—George Eliot

When you begin thinking about a new design, it's normal to think about ideas, concepts, and visual imagery. However, the first thing you do, before you even pick up a colored pencil, is think about the end of the process. Your final design is intended to be reproduced — maybe only 100 copies, maybe a few million. Either way, you need to consider the final end use of your work long before you put pencil to paper.

For the purposes of this chapter, we will assume that your designs have an unlimited budget. We will note where special budget considerations may be an issue, and some tricks to help out along the way.

Assuming you have complete creative control over your design, you have many decisions to make about the final product. What size will it be? What type of paper will you print on? What color paper? Should you use card stock? How can you make your product different than every other finished product out there? And how much will all this cost?

The Best Place to Start Is at the End

Design is only bound by one physical limitation — what the printer is able to reproduce. If your project is going to be printed on a desktop laser printer, you are restricted to something that fits on a letter-sized piece of paper (or possibly tabloid if it's a higher-end printer). Commercial printing is not so restrictive, though there are still some factors to consider.

For commercial graphic design, your only size limitations are what your printer can accommodate. Before you begin working on a concept, ask your printer if your idea is possible. Can their press handle a brochure that will have 18 × 24-in. spreads? Can they produce a mailing piece that is 5 inches high × 40 inches long, folded up to 5 × 5 inches? Your printer is always a good source of information, and should be able to answer your questions. (If they can't, perhaps you should find a new printer.)

When you're planning your final piece, you should be aware of the standard sizes of paper used by most commercial printers:

> 5.5 × 8.5-in. (Booklet)
> 8.5 × 11-in. (Letter)
> 8.5 × 14-in. (Legal)
> 11 × 17-in. (Tabloid)
> 25 × 38-in.
> 35 × 45-in.

European measurements are also frequently used in the design world, so you should be familiar with some of the most common:

Size	Inches	Millimeters	
A3	11.69 × 16.54	297 × 420	(Similar to tabloid)
A4	8.27 × 11.69	210 × 297	(Similar to letter)
A5	5.83 × 8.27	148 × 210	(Half-letter or booklet)
B3	13.9 × 19.68	353 × 500	
B4	9.84 × 13.9	250 × 353	
B5	6.93 × 9.84	176 × 250	

You can see from the list of standard paper sizes that more than one copy of a design can usually fit on a piece of paper. Designing for multiple-up imposition saves money on your final production costs. Paper is expensive. So if two copies of your design fit on a sheet of paper, you'll use half the amount of paper; four copies on the sheet cuts your paper consumption by half again, and so on.

If your final design is supposed to be a poster, your only concern about imposition is fitting the poster onto one of these sizes. Certain technical marks need to be incorporated onto a printed job, so keep in mind that a 25 × 38-in. sheet does not mean your poster can be 25 × 38-in. Find out from your printer the largest size piece they can produce, then go into the concept stage.

Multiple-up imposition. More than one of the same design can fit on a printed sheet.

A FEW WORDS ABOUT IMPOSITION

The final stage of the design process, directly before anything can be printed, is *imposition*. As a designer, it is not your responsibility to know how to execute imposition, or even to understand how the process works. But understanding the basic concept will give you an advantage.

Imposition refers to how the pages of a document are laid out on a printing plate in order to produce the final product.

A *signature* is a group of pages that are all printed on the same sheet of paper. That sheet of paper is then folded and cut to create the final brochure, catalog, part of a book, or other document. Pick up virtually any hardcover book and examine the top of the spine. You should see several different layers of what appear to be brochures, all bound together. Those are the signatures of the book.

To understand the general idea, take a plain piece of paper and fold it in half then in half again. Write the numbers 1 through 8 on your "pages" as you flip through; if you unfold the piece of paper you'll see that pages appear to be out of order and upside down. You have just created a *folding dummy* that shows how an 8-page brochure might be printed.

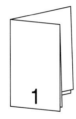

The "dummy" unfolds to show how an 8-page signature is laid out:

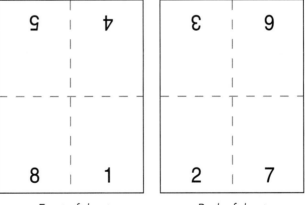

Front of sheet   Back of sheet

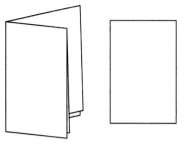

*This signature has eight pages.
The ninth page can't be bound in with the rest.*

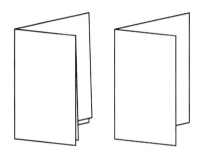

If you add a tenth page, the two can be bound into the middle of the first signature.

All you need to know about signatures is that they always have even numbers of pages (usually a number divisible by 4). If your final piece has seven pages, you will have a blank page that you're paying for anyway, so you might as well use it. If you design nine pages, you'll still end up with a blank page, as well as the considerable added expense of extra paper.

That's all you need to know about imposition. Of course, the more you know, the more valuable you will be in the marketplace.

SIZE DOES MATTER, ESPECIALLY TO THE POSTAL SERVICE

If your final product is going to be mailed, you'll have some additional restrictions to work with. The US Post Office has very specific guidelines about the weight, thickness, and flat size of anything that gets mailed. Consult your local post office for a guide to postal size requirements.

If you move outside of the USPS standards, your mailing costs can grow almost prohibitively. An excellent example of this is a company who designed a lovely holiday card measuring 5 × 5 in. Envelopes were not a problem, since most manufacturers either carry or can easily produce square envelopes. But no one thought to check with the post office before printing the cards. Three weeks after mailing over 200 cards, most of them were returned to the company for insufficient postage. (The company also found out, to their embarrassment, that some of the cards were delivered to very important clients — postage due.)

Of course, a square card would stand out from other standard sizes. But you need to evaluate the benefit of the additional mailing cost.

Paper Type, Color, and Texture

The paper you normally use in a laser or inkjet printer is around 20-lb. bond, 84% bright white. For a bit more money, you can upgrade to 24-lb. bond, 90% bright white. But what do those numbers mean?

All paper has several basic characteristics. *Paper weight* refers to the physical weight of 500 sheets at the paper's basic sheet size. If the paper mill cuts paper to the basic size of 25 × 38 in., then 500 of those sheets provide the paper weight: 20 lb., 80 lb., 100 lb., and so on.

Different papers also have different thickness and density, which means that 80-lb. book paper and 80-lb. cover stock are not the same thing. Cover (or card) stock is much bulkier and stiffer than book paper, even though both kinds of paper might have the same basic weight.

Optical properties of paper can be an important factor in your design. Papers have different levels of *whiteness*, *brightness*, *gloss*, and *opacity*. Consider clothing catalogs you get in the mail — high-gloss paper works well with the bright colors of the advertised products. But have you ever purchased a novel that was printed on glossy paper? Probably not. Gloss paper can be very straining on the human eye, so anything that will be read over extended periods should not be printed on gloss paper.

Paper can be coated to improve smoothness, brightness, ink absorbency, and gloss; or paper can be coated with a matte finish to reduce glare and gloss. Paper might have a textured finish, such as tweed, canvas, or "natural." Specialty paper finishes include vellum, parchment, recycled fiber, and countless others. (It would take an entire book to list every variation of paper that is available. This section only mentions a few examples of each variation.)

If selecting the right paper type isn't enough of a chore, you also have a virtually unlimited choice of paper color. Even white paper is not limited to white. There are many variations on the theme... bright white, soft white, white, white coated, gloss white, matte white, the list could go on.

Just visit an office supply store or quick printer and look at the different options. These retail outlets only carry what they can sell to the general public. A paper mill, on the other hand, offers even more options. Most paper companies will provide you with swatch books of the papers they offer, the different weights and thickness, and the colors that each of those are available in. Flip through any design magazine, and you will likely find full-page samples of different paper types.

Different paper color allows you to maximize the effect of your design. (We'll talk more about color in the next chapter, and how to use it effectively.) If you're trying to meet a low budget, but still want something different, consider printing one or two colors of ink on a light colored or "recycled" paper. If you can afford printing with high-opacity specialty inks or foil stamping, you may consider printing on a dark paper. Basic black conveys elegance, and could provide the impact you are looking for in an invitation, announcement, or other special design job.

Specialty paper can be very expensive. If your production budget is tight, you might ask your printer for suggestions. Many times printers have paper left over from another job that they will sell to you at a discount. Using this overstock is a great way to save money on a printing job.

The Right Paper for the Job

Design conventions usually specify certain types of paper for certain types of printing jobs. This is one area where you should stick to the conventions, since many of them are the result of practicality combined with years of research.

Books. The thickness of a book has to be considered. If a book has a high page count (such as phone directories, and encyclopedias), thick paper would make the book too large to be practical. The Yellow Pages for one section of Los Angeles is over 1,400 pages and weighs about four pounds. The next time you're in an office supply store pick up three reams of regular printer or copier paper. Can you imagine if this kind of paper was used in a phone book? Similarly, you wouldn't specify phone-book paper for a "high-traffic" or children's book, since it can be easily torn.

Packaging. Packaging material varies from clear plastic to cardboard. Paper selection depends largely on how the product will be displayed. Packaging design also has to consider resistance to cold (if it is a freezer case product), light resistance (stores usually have bright overhead lighting), and toxicity (if the paper is touching any kind of food).

Direct mail. Like size, the US Postal Service has very specific rules about the weight and thickness of anything you send in the mail. Postal rates are calculated by some cryptic equation relating weight and size; heavier paper will necessarily increase your mailing costs. Heavier or thicker paper might also increase the thickness of a final folded piece. Again, the Postal Service has standard rules about the thickness of mail.

High-traffic design. Maps, menus, and similar kinds of work require paper that can stand up to a lot of abuse. Menus and maps need to be sturdy enough to last for more than one use, and have a certain degree of wet strength. How useful would a map or menu be if the paper dissolved when it touched a drop of water? Both of these types of work also need paper with a high level of folding endurance. Maps need to be folded and (if you're lucky) refolded without ripping along the creases; menus should survive through more than one customer.

Periodicals and catalogs. Like direct mail, these projects use lightweight paper to keep mailing cost down. Catalogs and magazines are typically printed on glossy paper to enhance the appearance of advertising pages. Covers may be printed on a thicker stock to prevent ripping.

Postcards and reply cards. These projects always use paper thick enough to withstand mailing, usually 100+ lb. card stock (hence, the name). Reply cards might be uncoated, while postcards are usually higher-quality paper so that your family and friends can enjoy the true photographic beauty of your vacation destination. Business and greeting cards also use card stock, and can be glossy or not.

Stationary and letterhead. These types of design projects lean toward paper with a high cotton content or "linen" paper. Cotton-content paper is expensive, but presents an elegant and formal image.

Finishing Choices

Aside from binding, you have a number of options at the end of the production process. Folding, diecutting, embossing, foil stamping, lamination, and varnish each add different qualities to your finished design.

FOLDING

Have you ever opened a map, only to find that no feat of mechanical engineering can refold it to lie flat? Do you remember the skill and mastery it took to build a folded fortune teller in elementary school? There are several standard types of fold: gate, accordion, letter, over-and-over, and heads-in.

Of course these are not your only options. Standard practice lines up the edges and folds on the center- or the one-third line. But consider alternatives to the norm. If you can think of a way to fold it, it can probably be reproduced.

If you decide to use a fold in your design, keep in mind that there are special considerations involved with the finishing process. For instance, a three-panel gate fold will have one panel slightly narrower than the other two so that, when folded, the final piece will lie flat. Consult with your printer if you decide on folding; your printer is the best source for the technical specifications for your final design.

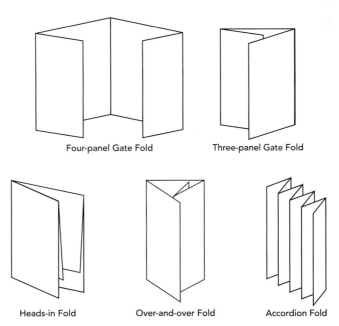

Four-panel Gate Fold   Three-panel Gate Fold

Heads-in Fold   Over-and-over Fold   Accordion Fold

DIECUTTING

Diecutting is another way to add style to your design. Paper doesn't need to be square, and doesn't need to have straight edges. Even something as simple as a tab within a brochure can draw attention to your work.

courtesy Impress Communications

Everything does not have to be a flat letter-sized piece of paper. These are just a few examples of unique diecuts and finishing options.

EMBOSSING, FOIL STAMPING, AND LAMINATION

Embossing and foil stamping can provide an elegant finish to your design. These are frequently used for invitations, letterhead, business cards, or formal announcements. Lamination is a good way to give your work a longer life. Menus and information cards are frequently laminated for protection, both from repeated use and from moisture.

VARNISH

Varnish might be used for several reasons. If you want a high-gloss appearance, varnish at the end of the printing run can add to the paper's gloss. Varnish also provides a certain amount of protection to the final printed piece; it can protect from wear-and-tear, and might also protect against water or chemical exposure. Spot varnish might be added to certain parts of a design to enhance or call attention to a particular area.

In Conclusion

There is no hard-and-fast rule that says everything you design has to be 8.5 inches wide × 11 inches high. In fact, even rotating the page orientation to 11 × 8.5-in. can make your work stand out. Of course, there are some conventions that you should at least pay attention to (booklets read front-to-back, left-to-right in the Western world), but in most cases the design police will not come after you if break from the mold. As a designer, it's your job to break from the mold!

CHAPTER 11

Using Pictures Effectively

*'What is the use of a book', thought Alice,
'without pictures or conversations?'*

—Lewis Carroll, *Alice's Adventures in Wonderland*

Pictures are used to help explain an idea, or to lend meaning to copy. The popularly held concept is that it takes years of disciplined study to master even the fundamentals of photographic technique. If you follow the guidelines listed below, your photographic skills will show dramatic improvement and your design projects will look more professional.

Picture Clarity

Picture clarity refers to both clarity of the idea and clarity of focus. When you are planning a photograph or photo shoot, think of exactly what you want to say about your subject. Weak photographs are usually weak because the photographer does not have a clear idea about the intent of the picture. One photojournalist stated that "fuzzy minds make fuzzy pictures."

For any design project, keep a "shoot list" of the photographs you will need. Before you begin clicking, consider the different possibilities for each image. If you're covering a function or event, compare the images you see and photograph with your shoot list; check off each item as you shoot it.

Clarity of focus is easier to accomplish than clarity of idea. A flash attachment or built-in flash will effectively freeze any movement, whether the movement is from the subject or the camera. Shutter speed at or above 100th of a second will also stop action. Many cameras also have an auto-focus feature. If you can't hold the camera still, consider using a tripod.

Photographers routinely use tripods for two reasons. You are almost certain to avoid camera-shake (especially with a large telephoto lens). More importantly, tripods guarantee that the area chosen for the picture (called framing the shot) will remain the same in every shot. The photographer determines the boundaries of the photograph and composes the elements within that "container." Once the shot is set up, the photographer can then concentrate on getting the right expression on the subject's face, or the perfect handshake, or the unexpected laughter.

Composition

There is a simple rule of composition for photography called the *rule of thirds*. If you divide a photograph into thirds with horizontal and vertical lines, the intersections of these lines mark the position for compelling photographic composition.

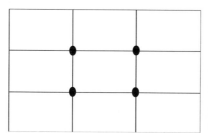

The rule of thirds. Place the subject at the intersections of the lines.

Notice how this picture uses the rule of thirds.

The framing coral leads the viewer's eye directly to the empty area. The composition is ready for a fish to swim perfectly into the frame.

Framing the Subject

It is a good idea to use elements to lead the viewer's eye into the picture. Use a tree limb, a doorway, a window frame, foliage, or similar elements to direct the viewer's attention to the subject. This technique also quickly establishes depth in the image, which is one of the powerful attributes of excellent photographic composition.

Move Closer

Some photographers claim that the most common photo technique problem stems from not getting close enough to the subject. People generally want to be as unobtrusive as possible when taking a picture. They usually do not "fill the frame" with their subject. Unless you eliminate distracting elements from the picture, the viewer will be unsure of the intent or the subject. At the risk of appearing too forward, move closer to your subject. Try this experiment: take a picture from where you would naturally

Picture taken too far away from the subject.

Closer shot provides better framing of the subject.

Best, most controlled cropping of the subject.

(Above) Typical poor composition.

(Right) Vertical composition moves this candid shot out of the amateur-snapshot realm.

stand. Then immediately move five to ten feet closer to your subject. Develop the film and compare the imagery. Which has more impact?

On the same subject of framing, many amateur photographers have a strange insistence on snapping horizontal images of people. Human beings are vertical subjects, so the camera should be held vertically — especially when taking headshot portraits.

Pictures of People

Most of the time, newsletters use photos of people to illustrate stories. Those pictures are almost always snapshots of an employee taken against a plain white wall, placed directly at the beginning of an article. By the time you get to the end of the article, no one remembers the face in the picture. With a little imagination, it is possible to turn unremarkable pictures into eye-catching design elements.

LINE OF SIGHT

If there is a person in the photo, use the direction of their gaze as an element of your layout. Use the subject's line of sight to move the reader through the layout.

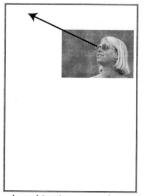

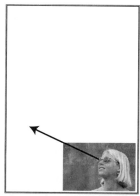

Using the subject's gaze to determine picture placement. The layout on the left directs the readers attention off the page. The layout on the right keeps the attention on the page, and moves the reader from the image into the text.

LAYOUTS FOR PEOPLE PICTURES

The size of a photo usually determines the importance of the subject. If you have a cluster of photos showcasing a team, the team leader should be larger than the other team members.

You might also use equal-sized photos, but this option is less visually stimulating. Don't fall into the trap of displaying a group of headshots in neat, predictable rows. Think of using the images to form an interesting, asymmetrical pattern. Use rules to organize the space as necessary.

It is immediately apparent from the size who is the team leader.

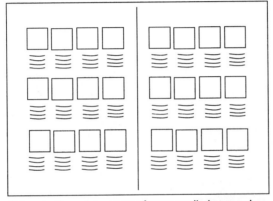

Unimaginative arrangement of many small photographs.

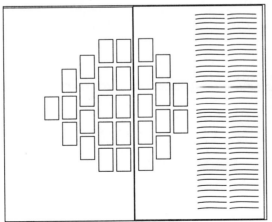

Better arrangement of small photographs.

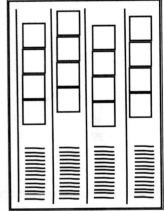

Use of rules to organize visual and written information.

Enhance Visual Impact

Desktop publishing offers a wide array of effects and treatments that, when used with discretion, can enhance your images and lend impact.

THE PHOTOGRAPH AS AN OBJECT

Present the photograph as an object. By enhancing the photograph itself, you create a visual interest in the picture. You can achieve this separateness from the column arrangement by tilting the photo at an angle on the page.

THE PHOTOGRAPH AS A FLOATING OBJECT

Make the photo appear to be a separate object hovering above the surface of the paper by creating a drop shadow.

Many graphics programs have a filter to makes the edge of a photograph look as if it were curled up.

(Top left) A page-curl filter applied to "lift" the image off of the page.
(Top right) Photograph with drop shadow.
(Bottom right) A simple vignette edge treatment.
(Bottom left) A textured edge adds interest to the picture of dolphins.

OTHER EFFECTS

Other effects can also add visual impact to your photographs. You might apply a special edge treatment to your photograph; styles range from simple vignettes to rustic or grunge edge treatments.

Other than simple edge effects, most graphic software provides a range of filters and effects to alter your photos. If you absolutely have to run a poor photograph, there are some simple, one-step filters that can dramatically improve the visual impact of the image. Depending on the software program you are running, the filters will be named differently; look for the function, rather than the exact name of the filter when locating it within your software.

Filters range from basic color changes, to embossing to different rendering of the photo. You can use graphics filters to make your photo look embossed, to turn it into a pen-and-ink or mezzotint type sketch, to blur the focus of some areas, or to achieve a range of other special effects. Find the filter that enhances your particular image without overwhelming it, but be sure not to get carried away with special effects.

The normal image, embossed, and ink outline filters.

PROJECTS

We have designed these projects to have the look and feel of real-world graphic design problems... something you would be likely to encounter in your work.

The following three projects are based on the work you have already completed in the Section 1 projects. If you did not complete those activities, you will need to revisit those as the basis of your work here.

The goal of these projects is to take a concept and work it through to the final product. The projects in Section 2 focus on applying what you've learned about the specific elements of design. If you haven't already done so, you will need to begin at the brainstorming step.

A New Face on Sunny Island

THE CLIENT SAYS:

We've done some market research and gotten feedback from the International Travel Agents' Association. They've all told us the same thing — that people don't want to just relax anymore. So we've slightly changed our focus and incorporated a variety of entertainment options for our guests. We still intend to promote ourselves as the ultimate relaxation getaway, but the brochures will have to mention some of the possibilities.

We need two marketing pieces: a brochure to send to the travel agents and an ad that will run in all the major travel magazines. The grand opening weekend is scheduled in two months, so we don't have a lot of time.

YOUR ART DIRECTOR SAYS:

We know they liked what you did for the logo, so maintain the same color scheme and feel in these projects.

The magazine ad is standard, but let's do something that will stand out from the crowd. Look through some travel magazines and see what other people are doing. Stay away from all the standard resort imagery — no palm trees, no silhouetted person laying in a hammock. You already have the slogan, which you can turn into a headline. We don't have any other copy right now, so why don't you try to come up with something. I'm leaving this entirely up to you. Once you've developed the layout, you will need to figure out what images you want from the client so their photographer can do a shoot.

We know they're willing to spend a lot of money, so we can do virtually anything for the brochure. I want to see two different concepts, and make sure you select a good paper to print on. The printer said they will need final artwork in three weeks if they're going to print, finish, and ship brochures to the travel agencies in time for the grand opening.

YOUR FINAL SUBMISSION:

Develop two different magazine layouts. If you include copy, you have to write it. Images can come from any source, including stock photography.

Also develop two brochure layouts. You have complete control of format, size, paper, and finishing. Budget is not an issue; but the less you spend, the more popular you will be with your client.

Reinventing the Zoo

THE CLIENT SAYS:

Congratulations, your logo and icons were the best ones — everyone else submitted computer-generated clip art of cartoon animals!

We need two things, rather quickly. First, we need an invitation to the formal ribbon cutting. The ceremony will be in one month, and we're really cutting this close. We actually already contacted everyone since it's so soon; we know who's going to be there, so this is really more of a reminder. It only needs to state the date, time, and location of the ceremony.

We also need thank you cards to send to all of the people who have donated time or money to helping us. We want the cards to be very artistic, something you could frame and hang on your wall. The only text should be: "In appreciation of all your help, Thank you." Make sure the logo is there, but it doesn't have to be too prominent.

Finally, we need a media kit we can mail. Since we'll be doing periodic press releases, we want a folder that we can print once and revise by changing the contents. We also want an informational brochure that describes the different sections of the park, the ones you designed the icons for. The brochure is going to go into every media kit, and will also be available at the gate for our visitors so it should have a map of the facility. Our first mailing will be a couple of weeks after the public opening so we have a little more time for this project.

YOUR ART DIRECTOR SAYS:

The two cards both need to be done quickly, but the invitation is definitely the most important. They need to mail in about two-and-a-half weeks so that they arrive before the ceremony. It sounds like they want more of a certificate than a thank you card; if they just wanted a plain thank you card they would go to the card store and buy a packet of them. Keep your designs close to a standard card size, but otherwise you can do anything to make it what they want.

Since they like the artistic look, stick with that for the folder design. Just get a plain folder from the supply cabinet and lay it out flat for the measurements. Make sure any area that is glued doesn't have ink on it, since the glue might not stick. The brochure should be one piece since it's going to be passed out at the gate of the zoo; a bunch of loose pieces of paper floating around the zoo won't make the environmentalists happy. Pick any format you like, but make sure you use the same artistic style on the folder and the brochure. Remember that the media kit is a unified piece, not just a folder with a bunch of stuff stuck into it.

YOUR FINAL SUBMISSION:

Create an invitation and a thank you card incorporating the logo and icons you already designed. Develop a media kit, including the folder and an eight-page brochure. Make sure you select the kind and color of paper for each, and the format for the brochure. Remember that a brochure doesn't have to be a flat piece of paper.

So Long, Crazy Harry

THE CLIENT SAYS:

We really like your work, but we're not quite there yet. I want the logo to use Roman columns surrounding the second name you came up with. I'll let you be the judge of how to arrange everything, but I definitely want the columns.

We need letterhead and business cards. I'll have two sales people, one general manager, one finance manager, and one office administrator. I only have the salespeople so far: their names are Bret Smith and Susan Jones. The rest will be hired as we go, so we'll have to do their cards later. I want the lot address on the cards, but I'm not sure where the office will be yet; use the lot address on the letterhead for now, but it may change.

We also need three different advertisements announcing our grand reopening. One will run in the local newspaper, one in the weekly entertainment tabloid, and one in the City Magazine. We're going to highlight a few of the available cars at the bottom of the ad but we haven't decided which ones to use yet. Just make sure there's room for at least two pictures and text. The main point of the ads, though, will be our new identity and the newly remodeled showroom. We'll get copy from the owner to you in the next week or so.

YOUR ART DIRECTOR SAYS:

I'm not sure that Roman columns are the best way to go for them since their new showroom is decorated in a very modern style. I'm guessing they saw the Roman Chariot dealership logo and liked the look. Why don't we try to incorporate the feel of columns into the business cards and letterhead instead of putting it directly into the logo? That will give them what they want. They're going to eventually need six business cards, but we only know two names so far. See if you can develop something we can print blank, then reprint with new names later. For the letterhead, just work with any address for placement, and we'll change the text once they decide where the office will be.

The ads are going to be more complicated. All three should have the same elements, but they're different sizes: One is a full-page newspaper size in black-and-white, one is a tabloid-size newspaper that prints with black and red, and one is a magazine size that prints four-color process on glossy paper. They want to highlight the new showroom, so we'll definitely want to use a picture. The introductory copy will come from the owner; for now just greek in about two paragraphs. People like to see their faces in print, so work a headshot of the owner into the layouts. As far as highlighting a couple of cars, it doesn't really fit but we can still work with it. Just use any picture you can find for placement.

YOUR FINAL SUBMISSION:

Using the "dignified" logo that you already created, develop templates for business cards (2 × 3.5-in.) and letterhead (8.5 × 11-in.) Develop three advertisements to intro- duce the new dealership identity:
- One black-and-white full-page newspaper ad.
- One two-color tabloid-size newspaper ad.
- One four-color magazine ad (8.25 × 10.5-in.)

SECTION 3

THE GRAPHIC DESIGN MARKETPLACE

Now that you've got all of the elements, what can you do with them? You know how to get an idea, how to develop it, and what to do to create the design. So what will you do with this information? The graphic design marketplace is broad and diverse.

"I'm a graphic designer." What does that mean? If someone says this, you probably will have a vague idea that they do something with art, but do you really know what they do? "Graphic design" is a very broad umbrella; it is similar to saying "I'm a consultant." Consultant for what? What do you consult about? What do you design for? Most graphic designers have a specialty in some particular aspect of the design industry. Some people are illustrators, some people work in advertising, others design Web pages.

For the beginning graphic designer, the most common mistake is to try to do everything. A little bit of illustration, some advertising design, a few packages, a logo or two, even a Web site thrown in to round out the portfolio. It is definitely good to have some experience in the different fields of design work. But as you progress through your career, it is always a good idea to find the particular field of design that you're best at, and specialize in that area.

Many times, your first job in the graphic design industry will be for a firm that services a wide range of clients. You might be asked to design a logo one day, and assemble a 200-page catalog the next week. Of course, it is always good to be able to switch modes, but most designers eventually find one particular aspect they really enjoy, and that they really excel at.

So who can you work for as a "graphic designer"? This industry has one of the broadest possible applications, which means that we can work for anyone. Every single company, in every possible industry, will at some point use graphic design. From the neighborhood diner's menu to a multinational corporation's product catalog to the local tourist center's Web site, all industries are affected by the graphic design market.

You might choose to work for a publisher, an advertising agency, an Internet company, a large corporation's in-house graphic design group, or even a printer. Regardless of which you choose, you should be aware of the different functions within any graphic design group, and the different fields of design that you might eventually specialize in. This section will break down the broadest fields of graphic design.

- Publications:
  Books, magazines, catalogs, annual reports, directories, and so on

- Illustration:
  Information graphics, editorial illustration, technical illustration

- Corporate identity:
  Logos, stationary, business cards, and so on

- Packaging:
  Labels, cans, boxes, wrappers, shipping cartons, display packaging, bags, music, and so on

- Advertising:
  Brochures, magazine ads, newspaper ads, direct mail, and so on

- Web design and Multimedia:
  Web sites, interactive kiosks, games, multimedia presentations

There are numerous books available that provide in-depth analyses of these categories, and even more specific ones written on the specialties within each. Our intention is to briefly describe your options, including some of the issues that are specific to those categories. We will also get some advice straight from the proverbial horse's mouth — seasoned designers who have worked in these industries for years. Finally, the Gallery of Graphic Design presents full-color examples of the different categories, with descriptions of how each project evolved.

Who's Doing What?

Before we examine the different categories of graphic design, you should be aware of the different roles people play in the graphic design market. Keep in mind as you read through these descriptions that many designers fill two or more job functions, depending on the size of the firm for which they work.

ART DIRECTOR

The art director (also sometimes called the design director or principal) is at the top of the graphic design food chain, and typically provides the backbone of any design group. This function is a combination of management and creative roles; the art director may be responsible for hiring new members of the group, maintaining project schedules, print buying, and client relations. They will also provide creative input for any or all projects in the workflow; depending on the person, he or she may retain complete creative control or simply provide advice when necessary.

The art director is the liaison between corporate management, client representatives, and the graphic designers working on a project. They will also communicate directly with the printer, paper supplier, and production house to make sure that projects are where they need to be, when they need to be there. The art director is also responsible for acquiring permissions to use copyrighted images, and for protecting the copyright on that group's work.

The art director position is not usually something you can simply decide to be; most companies prefer 10 or more years of experience in potential applicants for this position. Many schools provide classes specifically geared to the art director-in-training, adding business and management techniques to the traditional design curriculum.

HEAD GRAPHIC DESIGNER

The head graphic designer, depending on the size of the design group, is second in command, and is usually the designer with the most experience. The head designer might be responsible for delegating specific projects within the group, and could also lead brainstorming sessions for any or all projects. The head designer usually maintains his or her own projects, creating the concepts and artwork for use in a composition.

PRODUCTION DESIGNER

Once the head graphic designer has created a concept, the project may be handed off to a production designer. The production designer is responsible for creating the final printable document based on the head designer's concepts. If the project is created on a computer, the production designer makes sure that all the elements of a design are high-resolution printable files. The head designer might frequently work with low-resolution "for-placement-only" (FPO) files so that more time is spent designing and less is spent waiting for the computer to process large files. The production designer, then, is responsible for either adjusting or (more likely) recreating those low-resolution FPO files so that the elements will print cleanly.

LAYOUT ARTIST

We have stressed the fact that being a graphic designer does not require a savant-like ability to draw; layout artists exemplify this concept. Some graphic designers couldn't draw a stick figure if they had crayons glued to their hands, but their layouts look to be inspired by muses. Layout is a specialized skill that (like all of the elements we've discussed in the second section) can be learned; but unlike the other design elements, layout artists are hired specifically for that skill. (Have you ever heard of a "negative space artist"?) Layout artists are most commonly found in the publication sector of the graphic design industry, since books and other long documents revolve around page layout. Even with the most beautiful artwork, a publication is useless if the layout doesn't flow smoothly. This role is frequently considered a part of the "production designer" position; however, some groups have two different people.

IMAGING SPECIALIST

"Imaging specialist" is a broader heading for any of the following: scanner operator, photographer, color correction specialist, or similar specialists. Imaging specialists are responsible for (hence the name) acquiring the images to be used in a design project, whether through photography, scanning, or some other means. They are also responsible for preparing those images for printing, including color correction and retouching.

ILLUSTRATOR

The illustrator is usually a person from outside the design group who is hired to fill a specific need; once a project is complete the illustrator is off to find a new project. With the exception of some book publishers, most design groups do not hire a full-time illustrator. Illustrators are a very specialized group; they have their own trade organization, and generally have some specific area of knowledge to support their illustration work. Since this is both a job function and a field of design, we will discuss it in greater detail when we discuss the category of design called illustration.

PREFLIGHT OPERATOR (ELECTRONIC PREPRESS OPERATOR)

The preflighter (or prepress operator) is not necessarily a person who performs a graphic design function. In fact, many people don't even recognize the term. Prepress operators are the behind-the-scenes foundation of the graphic design world; very little would ever be printed without prepress. However, we argue that the preflight technician is one of the most important people in the graphic design workflow. It is also one of the most available jobs in the industry, since it is not the most flashy or the most recognized. Preflight operators do not win awards for their fine work, and are usually not even listed on the final run. But very little would get done without them.

Prepress operators are responsible for the quality control of graphic design. They are responsible for checking the work of the design department, making sure that files are the appropriate resolution, that all elements in a design are present, that the fonts are working properly, and a wide range of other technical issues. Graphic designers do not necessarily know the technical requirements of the projects they create; preflight operators are frequently required to fix the associated problems, which means that they must know the technical *and* design aspects of the industry.

COPYWRITERS, EDITORS, AND PROOFREADERS

Graphic designers do little, if any, writing. Most agencies and corporations hire specialists to write advertising copy for their products. If you work for a smaller group or decide to freelance, you may be called on to *help* write text; but you will rarely hear a client say, "Make me an ad. The content is entirely up to you." Once you've finished a design, it will usually be sent back to the original writer (even if the writer is the client) or editor to make sure the text is correct.

In chapter 4, Putting It All Together, we discussed the importance of carefully checking a proof so that errors do not get printed. Any design which includes text should be reviewed by a proofreader *even before it is proofed*, to avoid wasting the money, time, and consumables to make a second set of proofs.

SUPPORT ROLES

Aside from these roles, you may find other very specific roles that are closely tied to graphic design. The *production coordinator* shuttles jobs through the production process from original concept all the way through printing and binding. The *print buyer* works with production houses to find the best options, the best quality, and the best price for the project. The *sales representative* usually has the closest contact with the client, and is a good source for brainstorming ideas or feedback.

Of course, the lines between many of these roles become blurred depending on the size of the design group. If you're the brave sort who decides to freelance, you will be performing all of these functions. Many companies allow each designer to retain complete autonomy for specific projects, which means that you'll be doing the project management, creative work, and production for whatever project you're working on. Some groups keep the lines very clear, which means that if you are hired as a layout artist, you can plan on doing nothing but page layout until you are reassigned or you move on to another company.

Last, but certainly not least...

THE CLIENT

Never think that graphic designers operate in a vacuum. We do not sit down and decide to create something for no apparent reason. Every single project begins with *the client*. This point bears repeating. If you have no client, you will not be designing anything. If you are not designing anything, you are not getting paid.

The client hires you to solve a specific communication problem. You cannot simply go off and return three weeks later with your "finished" piece. The client will usually have ideas, favorite colors or fonts, or specific images they want to use. Don't just nod, go away, and ignore their comments when you begin working. And never, never tell the client that their ideas are bad ones. (This seems obvious, but it happens more than you would expect.)

You should maintain frequent contact with your client throughout the creative process. Some clients allow the designer considerable autonomy, but some prefer to micromanage the placement of every single line and letter on the page. Get to know your clients; learn as much as you can about their preferences and opinions. Once you develop a good working relationship, you will find that even the micromanagers will grow to respect your ability to find effective solutions, and will allow you more creative freedom.

The Next Step

You've already taken the first step by reading this book. There are numerous resources available to the beginning designer. The American Institute of Graphic Arts (AIGA) and the Graphic Artists Guild (GAG) are both valuable sources for industry information. Following is a list of books that are excellent additions to your library. If you can't buy them, check them out of a library and review the information, and take notes.

- *Graphic Artists Guild Handbook of Pricing and Ethical Guidelines*,
  Graphic Artists Guild, Inc., New York.
  Includes the latest industry standards for pricing your work;
  a complete guide to professional ethics and standards; clear
  explanations of the legal issues that affect graphic designers;
  and sample contracts for you to use.

- *AIGA Professional Practices in Graphic Design*,
  American Institute of Graphic Arts, New York.
  Detailed coverage of the practices and standards that govern
  the graphic design field, including designer-client relationships;
  management issues; marketing and publicity; rights; ethics; and
  environmental concerns.

- *AIGA Graphic Design: A Career Guide and Education Directory*,
  American Institute of Graphic Arts, New York.
  Defines the purpose and practice of the field and identifies the
  links between effective educational programs and professional
  practice. Provides helpful advice about what employers look for
  in prospective employees.

- *Artist's and Graphic Designer's Market*,
  Writer's Digest Books, Cincinnati.
  Provides valuable industry information about how and where
  to sell your work. Lists publishers in different categories that buy
  art and design work; includes address and contact information
  for each publisher, as well as the publisher's specific needs and
  requirements.

CHAPTER 12

Publication Design

It is to be noted that when any part of this paper appears dull there is a design in it.

—SIR RICHARD STEELE (*THE TATTLER*)

Publication design comprises a wide range of design projects — books, magazines, newsletters, newspapers, reports; anything more than a few pages might be considered a publication. Depending on the specific type of publication, the design could be as simple as typesetting hundreds of pages of a novel, or as complicated as designing a full-color "coffee table" book.

Whatever type of publication design you are working on, you will likely have little control of the content. You probably won't get to choose the illustrations, since the publisher has probably already commissioned the appropriate artwork. You may have some creative input for the cover art or a few pages within the book. But more likely your job in this field will be to implement a layout design that works for that particular type of publication.

Publication design is not the specialty for everyone. If you prefer exercising your drawing ability, or would rather spend time developing illustrations and images, then you should explore other options. However, if you find that you have a flair for creating layouts, publication design may be the specialty for you.

Specialties within Publication Design

Most publications are designed with the general public in mind, which means that the design is not governed by a specific set of rules. There are, however, several special markets within the category of publication design: children's, scientific and technical, educational, and art. Each of these special categories has more specific design requirements.

Children's publications typically use larger type, less words on a single page, wider leading between lines of type, shorter column widths, and more illustration. Children's publications, especially for the very young, use bright or vibrant colors and realistic images to reinforce the message of the text. This specialty is very detail-oriented since the design needs to tell the story for children who can't or are only just learning to read.

Art publications are heavily illustrated, and may have little or no text. Design work for these publications is an art itself. The most important thing is to emphasize the images, with very small type and minimal interruption. Publishers in this field focus on clean, elegant layout, without anything floating on a page which might distract from the topic.

Scientific and technical publications tend to have the most type and least illustration, use smaller type sizes and longer column widths, and place more emphasis on the content rather than the design. This is not meant to say that this kind of publication is design-free, only that the design is usually very simple and free of extraneous elements.

Educational publications (textbooks, newsletters, and the like) vary depending on the subject matter and intended audience. This kind of publication gives you the advantage of immediately knowing your target audience, which gives you a head start on your layout. Texts for younger children (elementary to middle school) follow the same criteria as children's publications — larger type, shorter columns, more illustration. High school and college texts are more text-heavy, and might have little or no illustration (there aren't too many exciting images that go along with, say, calculus.)

Publishers who specialize in any of these categories prefer designers who also follow that specialty. If your experience is mostly in educational publishing, you may find it hard to break into the art publishing world.

Many publishers have a specific template for their publications. Users will know exactly what to expect when they open a different book within the same series, which is especially important for educational texts.

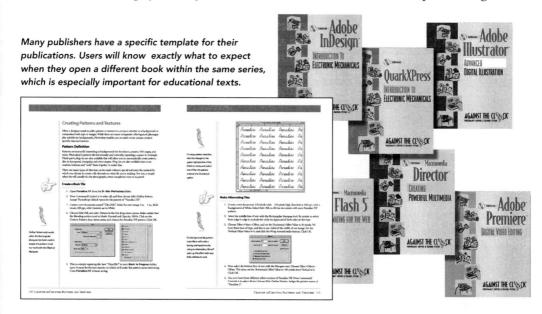

Advice from...
Marianne Frasco, *Design Manager, Prentice Hall*

A good textbook design combines a balance between esthetics and functionality. Both the design and the printed information have to work together so that students reading the book get a clear sense of order and organization. Visuals are meant to help guide the learning process and must work in a clear and concise manner with the text material.

A good textbook designer knows how to present visuals and combine them with text in a way that is visually exciting and inviting to the reader without overkill. When hiring a designer we look first for a great portfolio. Just as important as the portfolio is the way the designer executes the assignment. This includes excellent technical skills. Keeping up with new software and software extensions is important because it enables the designer to stretch the limits of design.

If you are used to designing technical publications, you may find children's work a difficult switch. Each of these specialties has a very different set of guidelines and requirements, so go with what you're good at, and what you enjoy.

Many designers in these niche markets have a strong background in that specialty. How would you know what a delta symbol should look like if you've never heard of one? If you have no idea what an isotope is, how would you draw the subject matter for a radioactive isotope magazine into your page layout? Of course these are very specific examples, but a small amount of knowledge goes a long way in creating effective layout designs. Of course, you should learn about your subject regardless of the type of publication you are working for. Desktop publishing software makes it very easy for practically anyone to arrange text on a page; but the professional designer will do the research and create a layout that makes the text and the subject matter come alive.

SPECIAL MARKETS — CATALOG DESIGN

Catalogs are a very unique beast in the design world. If you walk into any design firm or ad agency, you'll probably see people throwing a large catalog project at each other in a "hot potato" routine. Many designers get a catalog assignment, cringe, and hide under their desks because the work is time consuming, very detail oriented, sometimes a bit monotonous, and not overly glamorous. But quality catalog design is vital for any company that sells something. Especially in the retail world, hundreds of thousands of dollars are spent creating inviting, attractive catalogs.

A catalog is, to a designer, a multi-page jigsaw puzzle. It's your job to fit five lines of type into space for three, and fit seven products onto a page designed for six. The final piece has to be organized, logical, readable, and attractive all at the same time. Successful catalog designs rely on your ability to use layout as an art form — the layout itself is the "design" because the point is to highlight the product. If you are good at designing catalogs, you'll find no shortage of work.

courtesy Impress Communications

In chapter 6, Layout, we showed one of the master pages used to create a 120-page catalog. The images here are from the same project.

In total, this project incorporated 12 sections, 14 different master page layouts, 23 predefined style sheets, nearly 380 images, and over 1000 products. The project went through 7 client revisions, and took nearly 250 hours to complete.

Hints for Successful Publication Design

No matter what publication you're designing, select one or two font families for the entire project. It's fine to use variations of the same font (within reason); but the only time you should ever use more is if you're designing a book about fonts. If you've got 28 different fonts in your book, you've crossed the line.

Use the same layout for every chapter in a book, and for every page in a magazine or newsletter. This does not mean that every single page has to have three columns of type and a picture stuck right in the center. But use the same colors, margins, and styles throughout an entire publication. If you have a number of call-outs or sidebars, every one of them should have the same general appearance — if one has a bounding box they all should, and if one has a shaded background they all should. You might use different colors for the box or background, but the percentage and line width should be consistent. This gives the whole project unity, which is as important for 2-page newsletters as it is for 800-page books. If a publication doesn't have a unified look and feel, the reader might get confused or annoyed and throw it away. This doesn't make the publisher happy, which means you don't get the next job.

Remember that we discussed the basics of *imposition* in chapter 11, Using Pictures Effectively. All publications work on the concept of printed signatures; there will always be an even number of pages, usually in multiples of 8 or 16. If you've finished designing your book and you only have 275 pages, you will probably have 5 or more blank pages somewhere in your book (275 pages divided into 8-page signatures = 34 signatures plus 3 extra pages, which means you need 5 more to make that final signature).

Breaking into the Market

Many publishers have an in-house staff of designers. Magazine publishers spend thousands of dollars to develop their format, and once it's done they usually stick with it for a while. Book publishers often have a template for their publications, and new titles are dropped into that template, fine-tuned, and printed.

Publishers may, on occasion, commission independent work, either to accommodate overflow from the in-house staff or to create a new look. There are a few independent firms which specialize in publication design, but this is much less common.

If you want to specialize in publication design, your best place to start is to work in-house for a local publisher. Once you've gained experience, you'll have a better chance of getting freelance assignments.

START SMALL, START LOCAL

Another option for breaking into the field is to work with small local groups and organizations. Most communities have civic groups, special interest organizations, or a visitor's association — and all of these groups produce publications. Local organizations, as a matter of civic pride, generally prefer to work with local designers. Your city's Chamber of Commerce is a great source of information if you decide on this route.

Even if it's only a small black-and-white newsletter at first, you may find more opportunity for this kind of work. Once you've completed a few small projects and built a local reputation, you may find that the larger projects — full-color catalogs, event programs, directories, or magazines — are yours if you want them. You'll also find that word of mouth is better than any kind of advertising you could buy. If your clients are happy, they'll tell their friends.

CHAPTER 13

Illustration

To envision information — and what bright and splendid visions can result — is to work at the intersection of image, word, number, art.
—EDWARD TUFTE, *ENVISIONING INFORMATION*

Illustration is a very unique animal in the graphic design industry. The word illustration encompasses so much, yet is perhaps as vague as the concept of "graphic design." So what is illustration? We've already briefly discussed the possibility of choosing the profession of an "illustrator" as your intended career path — that's one possible definition of the word.

Illustration, as a category of design, can be roughly broken down into two subcategories: information graphics and editorial illustration. The following section looks at these two fields. We will provide a brief definition of each field, and discuss the uses and possibilities of this career specialty.

Information Graphics

Information graphics (often abbreviated to "infographics") are created to display information in some visual manner other than text. This kind of illustration is frequently used in newspapers, magazines, scientific publications, presentations, and in any number of other places. Information graphics are generally used to visually represent complex statistics, numerical or scientific data, or some other item that benefits from a pictorial description. Information graphics range from simple pie charts and line graphs to elaborate full-color images and detailed maps. Many signs also fall under the information-graphics heading.

Notice that "information" is the first word in information graphics. Also notice that this category is not called "information decorating." The information is the priority. Of course, you will give consideration to the visual appeal of what you create; but the integrity of the information is the most important aspect of creating information graphics.

EARLY INFORMATION GRAPHICS

An early example of information graphics best illustrates the value of presenting complex statistical information in a visual way. In the 1890s, London was overwhelmed by a large number of deaths with no known cause. Comparisons of age, occupation, ancestry, and recreational habits showed no correlation, so the town councilors organized the deaths by residence. Using a large street map of the city, they placed pins at the location of each victim's house. This organization of the data showed that every victim's house was built on the marshy land within two blocks of the docks — a common thread that tied the seemingly unrelated deaths together. This lead to the discovery that drinking water in that specific area was contaminated by refuse dumped into the Thames River. Without graphical representation of the data (the pins in the map), the town leaders might never have noticed the connection.

THE IMPORTANCE OF INFORMATION GRAPHICS

Information graphics have recently become more important because there is simply too much information out there for us to assimilate. Very few people have time to read an entire article in the newspaper, not to mention reading a magazine cover-to-cover. Information graphics take the information contained in an article or story, condense it, summarize it, and present it in a manner that takes (usually) seconds to comprehend

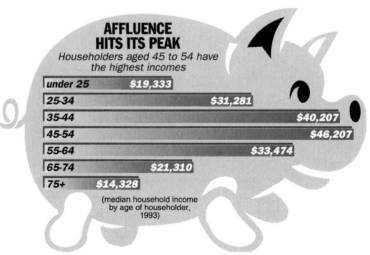

This type of information graphic, created by Scott MacNeil, presents statistical information in a more appealing format than a simple list of numbers. The piggy bank background adds an illustrated element to attract the readers' eye.

instead of minutes or hours. The next time you open a newspaper or magazine, flip through it and pay attention to the graphics (not just the pictures). You'll probably be able give a fairly accurate summary of the articles contained within, without reading a single paragraph of copy. Information graphics make it easy to digest information and understand relationships within the presented data.

Newspapers and magazines use information graphics for several reasons:
- To simplify detailed information
- To distill information that might otherwise take "too long" to read
- To attract interest so that the reader will read the whole article
- To break up long blocks of black-and-white text

If you are able to distill information quickly, you may have a good choice of careers in information graphics. Because of the quick turnaround time for most newspapers and magazines, this kind of design has to be done very quickly. You might be given an article at 6 a.m. and be expected to deliver your graphics by 4 p.m. to meet the press time for the morning edition. Speed, as well as accuracy, are both important in this field.

ETHICAL CONSIDERATIONS

Staistical data is a concrete thing, which means that you cannot take creative liberty with its visual representation. Researchers who take liberties with their data find themselves quickly out of work or worse; you'll experience the same trouble if you manipulate the visual representation. Information graphics should be factual and accurate. Scale, proportion, and similarity of units should all be exact. If you're creating a graph or chart to compare amounts, be certain to clearly illustrate the relationship.

When comparing measurements, keep the units consistent for each amount represented. Convert dissimilar units to the common one. For example, kilometers are (numerically) larger than miles. If one item of your chart is labelled "27 kilometers" and another is labelled "18.6 miles", the reader may not know that the two are the exact same distance. Convert miles to kilometers (or kilometers to miles), but always use the same measurement within a graphic so that the reader is not mislead.

Technical Illustration

Technical illustration is a specialized segment of editorial illustration. Now that it seems the whole world is "High-tech," this kind of illustration is more prevalent in just about every area of graphic communications. Technical illustration includes schematics, diagrams, charts, and maps; work could be as simple as a line drawing to illustrate product assembly, as complicated as a highly detailed drawing of an interior combustion mechanism, or anything in between.

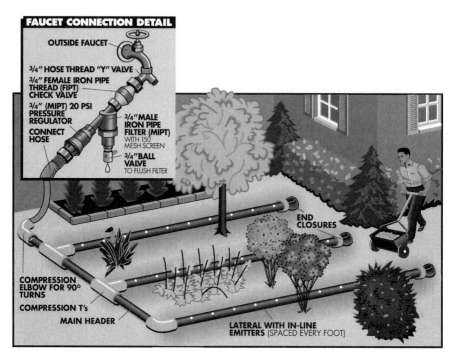

FAUCET CONNECTION DETAIL

OUTSIDE FAUCET

3/4" HOSE THREAD "Y" VALVE

3/4" FEMALE IRON PIPE THREAD (FIPT) CHECK VALVE

3/4" (MIPT) 20 PSI PRESSURE REGULATOR

CONNECT HOSE

3/4" MALE IRON PIPE FILTER (MIPT) WITH 150 MESH SCREEN

3/4" BALL VALVE TO FLUSH FILTER

END CLOSURES

COMPRESSION ELBOW FOR 90° TURNS

COMPRESSION T's

MAIN HEADER

LATERAL WITH IN-LINE EMITTERS (SPACED EVERY FOOT)

This illustration by Scott MacNeill makes installing a home sprinkler system much more easy to understand. Technical illustration is useful from the basics of a faucet hookup to the complexities of an internal combustion engine.

This kind of work requires attention to detail, thorough knowledge of the subject matter, and the ability to communicate very complex ideas graphically. Technical illustrators usually have some background in science or technology. As practically everything around us becomes more technical, the need for technical illustration will continue to grow.

Editorial Illustration

Editorial illustration differs from information graphics, since it is not intended to be an exact depiction of specific facts. Editorial illustration, works from the concepts presented in the text to enhance the information, or as a visual depiction of a story without any accompanying text. Editorial illustration ranges from book covers to editorial cartoons to posters; you have far more creative control over this kind of work, since you don't have to worry about inadvertently misrepresenting data.

DEFINING YOUR STYLE

When an editor hires you, they are hiring you for your style. They are counting on you to present work that repeats the certain look of your illustrations. It is important to have a strong, well-developed style. Your portfolio should include several pieces with the same treatment or feel, to show editors that the work they like is not just a fluke. This consistency demonstrates that you have a definable style, and that you can use that style effectively in a variety of pieces.

Initially, an editor will look at your existing artwork and buy the rights to use it in a specific way. For example, a health magazine might frequently run articles on the importance of nutrition. If you have several pieces dealing with this topic, you improve the odds of selling your work. The editor might even buy multiple pieces to guarantee continuity over several issues. Once you've proven yourself in the field, you may even be commissioned to create specific pieces.

Many editors contract on a *work-for-hire* basis. They assign you an article to illustrate, you design the illustrations for a set fee, and you get paid. In this scenario, the contracting client owns the illustration and can use it

Illustrators are usually hired for their personal style. These graphics, created by Don Morris, all have the same feel.

whenever and wherever they wish with no further payment to you. This, of course, benefits the magazine, and it is the best approach for new illustrators. After you've gained some experience and standing in the field, you will have more strength to negotiate your own advantage through a *limited usage* contract. This type of arrangement stipulates that the contracting agent (the editor) can use the illustration for specific purposes for a specific length of time. You agree that the client has the exclusive right to use that illustration for the limited time of the contract. The advantage here is that you can resell the illustration after the time limit has expired, whether to the same client or to a different one.

EDITORIAL ILLUSTRATION SPECIALTIES

Book covers. There is some debate in the industry about how to classify book covers; some covers are purely photographic, others are entirely fine art using traditional media, others are computer-generated design work. Even though some work might fall into the "fine art" category instead of "graphic design," we've placed book covers in the category of editorial illustration, since (whatever form they take) they do illustrate the concept of the text.

Every time a book is published, it needs to have a cover. Whether it's a textbook, a children's book, or a trade paperback, you have to put some image on the front. If you have the opportunity, look at a copy of *Artist's and Graphic Designer's Market* (it doesn't matter what year) under the "Book Publishing" section. Read through a few of the entries; most publishers accept submissions for cover art in their particular genre. Depending on the kind of book, different publishers may look for very specific styles of art — some prefer realism while others want a more impressionist look. Some publishers want photography, others won't use photos at all. There are even certain publishers who refuse anything created on a computer— your chance to put all those oil painting lessons to good use!

The best way to get an idea of a genre's style of illustration is to simply visit a bookstore. Go to the "Science Fiction/Fantasy" section. Pick up any book there, and you'll be looking at one of the most specialized categories of editorial illustration. Science fiction book covers usually incorporate realistic-looking, highly detailed artwork. Next, move over to "Romance." These books almost always have very realistic images of people in detailed settings; the covers are (usually) created from paintings, which (believe it or not) use real people as models. Find a Harlequin historical romance on the shelf, and you're likely going to find a painting or pastel drawing that someone got paid to create.

These are only two genres of books that need covers, but they are the ones with the most specific requirements. In fact, science fiction book covers have evolved to now be considered art genre in itself. There are awards devoted solely to excellence in this genre, and you can even buy books full of the "Best of...". Some people base their entire career out of science fiction illustration.

Advice From...
Don Morris, *Art Director, St. Petersburg Times*

Recognized as one of the nation's top ten newspapers, the St. Petersburg Times has built its long-standing reputation through a combination of hard-hitting editorial and compelling graphics.

In a sense, you're talking about apples and oranges when you compare editorial and informational graphics. Editorial graphics are more emotional; they're designed to get the reader/viewer more involved with the story in a subtle, tactile manner. They're meant to evoke feelings or create a mood.

Informational graphics are factual. They support the argument or position presented in the article or on the Web page clinically; "and to prove what we're saying, here are the numbers."

Whether you're talking about photographs, charts, or cartoons, the purpose of the illustration is what causes it to fall into one or another category.

You're either trying to make them relate to the story or you're showing them the numbers.

Magazines. periodicals, brochures and reports use editorial illustration to enhance the text. From an editor's point of view, a good illustration should be an invitation to read the article. It should encourage the viewer to pause and read, as well as to convey some facet or theme within the article. Magazines have individual preferences for the types of illustrations they use. Certain news magazines, for example, expect their illustrations to be cutting, insightful commentaries on the articles they illustrate. The editors expect and desire political humor or visual sarcasm from their designers.

Fashion and beauty, home, health, and family magazines have a far different criteria for illustrations. Editors prefer more pastel or desaturated colors, open linework, have more airy treatments to the artwork. Emotional content of the design should be kept light.

Magazines geared toward men (like sports or car magazines) typically use a bolder, brighter range of color, have a stronger use of line, and have a tendency to illustrate the most basic theme of an article. The illustrations are not meant to be deep or intellectual. If your personal style is straightforward, and you gravitate towards a primary-color palette, this is the venue for you!

Many other special-interest magazines are being published today, ranging from science fiction to psychology to coin collecting. Each favors a different style of illustration, and each has a very pointed target market.

Posters and Calendars. Posters and calendars form a part of the editorial illustration industry. People buy calendars, of course, for the dates, but also as an affordable wall decoration. Calendar illustrations indicate a person's interests or hobbies, or may represent a "mini-vacation" — looking at a serene beach sunset on a calendar is a refreshing break from the ordinary especially when it is blustery and snowing outside. Most of the editorial rationales and business practices in this field are identical to those in magazine work. It is even more important, for this field, to present a coherent, strong individual style of work.

Calendars, by their nature, need 12 illustrations. Of course, it's very important to present a themed, unified set of 12 pieces. Calendar illustrations need to be appropriate for the months they represent, perhaps not in direct correlation, but there should be some association whether in color, imagery, or treatment. Calendar publishers work well in advance of the year's end, so it is best to call them and ask for the submission deadline for the next calendar. It might be almost a year in advance, so January is not too soon to make the call.

A promotional poster can be used to announce an event, festival, gallery opening, rave, movie, sporting event, or musical performance. Posters are a stylistic blend of word and visual, with two purposes: First, posters announce the event and inform the viewer of the particulars, such as location and date. Second, posters visually sum up the attitude or feel of event, and entice the viewer to attend.

The client is the person or company sponsoring the event; they are as diverse as the events being announced. However, they all have the same need: to catch the viewer's eye, and to inform the public. The latter is as important to the client as a great image. Promotional posters should have clean, easy-to-read, information-bearing text. The date, location, time, and any price should be instantly visible.

Art posters have specific criteria, and their popularity is based largely on current fashion. Trends in popular paint colors, upholstery colors, and accessory styles greatly influence which posters are going to sell. For example, interior color schemes featured dark green and rose accents a few years ago; posters utilizing those colors were popular. When the trends shifted to prefer desaturated, darker, and more complex color schemes, the green/rose color palette became dated.

Just as color is an important issue in the salability of poster art, so is style. Posters created for a mass audience must appeal to a wide range of tastes; the style has to be pleasing to many different tastes, and has to work with different interior styles. Once again, themed sets have better marketability than individual posters, especially in commercial spaces like hotels and office buildings.

The art poster industry has a booming market as framed prints. Every interior decorator and frame shop has books of inexpensive posters to decorate interior spaces. There are many different poster publishers, and they often specialize in specific target markets. For instance, some publishers only publish florals and landscapes. Others cater to the baby and children's market. Still others publish fantasy and science fiction. There is a niche for all types of illustrations in this field.

Breaking into the Market

There are many books published with specific information on how to approach this illustration market. You should also review design annuals from most of the trade magazines. If possible, invest in a copy of the *Artist's and Graphic Designer's Market*; this book is published every year, and contains the different categories of editorial illustration, the different publishers within the categories, and the contact person, submission requirements, and types of work each publisher uses. Because of the specific information listed in these volumes, you should buy a new copy every couple of years if possible.

The Society of Illustrators is a professional organization catering to working illustrators. The Society is an invaluable resource for industry news and business practices, and provides job boards, annual showcase books, and awards. The group's Web site hosts many networking and business opportunities, and provides advice to illustrators.

CHAPTER 14

Corporate Identity

'In politics,' said John Lindsey, *'the perception is the reality.'*
So, too, in advertising, in business, and in life.

—AL RIES AND JACK TROUT, *POSITIONING: THE BATTLE FOR THE MIND*

Logos, logotype, trademarks... whatever you call it, corporate identity is a multimillion dollar business. Millions of dollars are spent every year creating corporate identity. Depending on the size of the company, a single logo might cost between $3,000 and $200,000 (from the *GAG Handbook of Pricing and Ethical Guidelines*, 9th edition.) That's just for a logo! Add in the design for letterhead, business cards, presentation materials, and the like, and you can see just how important corporate identity is in the graphic design world.

Now consider that every company has a logo. And for every product that company creates, some designer is getting paid to develop a brand identity, which is another term for "logo." Walk down the cereal aisle the next time you're in a grocery store. How many different boxes have the General Mills logo on them? Probably at least 10 of the most popular cereals, and a few of the less-known ones. Every one of these brands has its own look, its own easily recognizable characteristics. That means that General Mills not only paid for the corporate logo, but also for each of these separate brand logos. The same is true for clothing, cars, and any other corporation with two or more "brands."

The most important feature of a good identity is that the viewer remembers it. Think of a few corporate logos that you know of. What do you remember about them? Why? We discussed, in the symbolism chapter, the instant recognition of successful logos... even if the whole image isn't there. Marketing experts spend countless hours and fortunes trying to plant their brand at the top of the consumer's mind. Since our culture responds most easily and quickly to visual cues, the logo for a product is one of the keys to that top positioning.

Hallmarks of Good Logos

A good logo has the following characteristics:

- It reinforces the "personality" of the product or corporation. It is witty where appropriate, formal where that trait enhances the respectability of the client.
- There are no extraneous elements.
- Color is used to reinforce the concept, but a logo must work in black-and-white.
- Type is chosen with skill
- The craft is immaculate (even if the corporate identity is gritty — the craft of "grittiness" is perfect).
- The logo would look great in a variety of media.
- The logo will work well at both large and small sizes.

The Client Is Always Right?

When you take on a logo-design project, the client is likely to say one of two things:

"I DON'T KNOW WHAT I WANT. I'LL KNOW IT WHEN I SEE IT."

This doesn't give you much to work with, other than the client's name. Sit with your client and listen to their input. Ask questions:

- Who is the customer?
- Who is the competition?
- Where is the product sold?
- What demographic is the client trying to reach?
- What type of image does the client want to portray (serious, silly, traditional)?
- What colors do they like?

When the client doesn't really know what they want, don't spend too much time on the design before you present your ideas. A New York dentist hired a designer to create an identity for his new office. The designer assumed that a dentist would want to convey trustworthiness and conservative values in the business presentation. Over the course of two weeks, several different traditional, stable, honorable, and conservative designs were submitted. Every one was rejected. This client exhibited every hallmark of the typical "know what they want when they see it."

Through interaction with the client, the designer eventually realized that the dentist practiced a rather flamboyant alternative lifestyle. The next design submitted was a hot-pink and purple card with punk-style type proclaiming him "the Manhattan Tooth Fairy." He loved it.

Advice from...
Andy Bing, *Owner, Bing! Design*

When I take on a new project, I talk with the client and find out what kind of business they own. I design six to eight completely different logos with a computer, which makes it easy to do multiple renderings. You can never tell how long this will take — sometimes the whole thing is finished in an hour, sometimes it takes a month to get it right.

I present the different concepts to the client; usually they like certain elements from each of the concepts. After this presentation, I go back to the computer and use the elements they like from each to create a final logo.

The logo for Bobby Rubino's® restaurants is a great example of this. I created these six initial concepts and presented them to the client. They chose the elements they liked from each design, which I incorporated into the final logo.

One thing to remember is that a logo needs to be placed on something, like a building, a sign, or a corporate stationary package. The layout for these things is a separate billing issue, but it's best to present a logo being used in some way.

I placed the final Bobby Rubino's® logo on sample stationary and a poster to give the client an idea of how it would look when it was really used at two very different sizes. This is much more effective than just an enlarged rendering floating on black artboard. Try not to make the client do too much work.

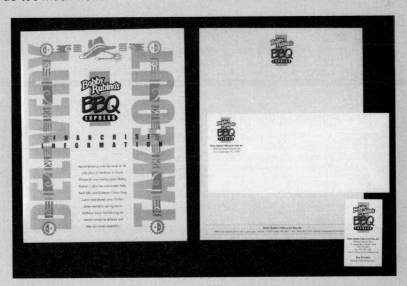

In this case, the designer was working on the wrong assumption — to create a respectable image; the client, though, wanted to appeal to a totally different client base. Know the purpose of the design before you get too far off track!

"THIS IS EXACTLY WHAT I WANT..."

The client walks into your office and says, "I want a vivid red background with a swirly line down the middle and our company name in script next to the line." Obviously, this situation presents a few problems. This kind of client is basing their plan on a logo they've seen and can remember (in this case, Coca Cola). Second, the red-background-white-swirl logo has nothing at all to do with the client's business. It certainly doesn't say that the company, for example, is a new Mexican restaurant.

by Liesel Donaldson

These images were generated during a brainstorming session to develop a logo for a new series of educational videos from a bridge design firm (Figg Engineers). The top three images visually incorporate kids and knowledge, and each solves the visual communication problem effectively. However, the "Segments of Knowledge" was chosen as the final logo, and bears little resemblance to the original ideas — proving that your initial concepts may not provide the final solution.

Your job, as a designer, is to persuade the client why they should not use the red swirly logo. Rather than arguing with the client about copyright violations (which you might come dangerously close to if you *do* recreate Coke's logo), take this idea and use it to brainstorm new ideas. Always listen to the client's input. Remember that it's not your logo, and you're not paying your own fee. Develop alternative design concepts that you think will better solve the client's problem, and be prepared to explain why you created what you did. You'll likely find that the client is happy. Many times they say they want something specific only because they've seen it before, and can't think of anything else. When you present good alternatives, they're impressed and happy.

If the client absolutely insists on using the red swirly design, you would be better off dropping the project. Most logos are copyrighted, and many companies are fiercely protective of those rights. If you steal someone else's look, you and your client could be heavily fined, not to mention the permanent damage to your professional reputation that you will incur. No client is worth *that* risk.

A second variation of this problem is the client with a three-page list of items to include in the logo. A new clothing reseller, The Treasure Chest, hired a designer to create a company logo. The client insisted on using the obvious "wooden treasure chest overflowing with clothing" image. The designer created the image, using abstracted articles of clothing inside an antiqued wooden box line drawing. The client loved it, except...

The client returned the first proof, she wanted the clothing to be more realistic. The designer made the clothes more realistic. The second proof came back with specific items of clothing to put in the box — a child's dress, a man's shirt, a woman's blouse, and a boy's jumper. Against better judgement, the designer sent the third proof with the specific clothing; it came back, and the client wanted to add address and contact information to the image.

You may imagine that this went on for a few more rounds, until the logo was far beyond the scope of a logo... the detailed line work, small text, and numerous elements worked very well as a poster, but could never be reduced, printed in black-and-white, or used for any purpose other than one poster.

If you encounter this situation, you have three options:

1. Try to explain that a logo has to work in many ways, at many different sizes, and in both color and black-and-white.

2. Put up with the endless changes, keep your complaints to yourself, and finish the job as quickly as possible.

3. Drop the project and cut your losses.

Depending on how open the client is to suggestion, you have to determine which of these solutions is the best in your situation.

CHAPTER 15

Point-of-Purchase Display and Packaging

Shoppers and moviegoers do not know capitalism... from the standpoint of plummeting prime interest rates and spurts in the Gross National Product, but rather from the perspective of the sensations caused by the vibrant colors of labels, the enticing rhetoric on packages, and the dewy-eyed beauty of actresses in romantic comedies.

—DANIEL HARRIS, *CUTE, QUAINT, HUNGRY, AND ROMANTIC: THE AESTHETICS OF CONSUMERISM*

The most powerful type of advertising is not television, print, billboards, radio, or the Internet. That distinction belongs to the specialized area of *point-of-purchase* (POP) display, which influences more purchase decisions than any of the other types. Studies show that over 40% of the decisions to purchase one brand over the next are made in the store. POP refers to advertising created for use at the point when a purchase can be made; like in a store or at a vending machine. This industry is the fastest growing of the major advertising and marketing disciplines. Because it is a $9 billion a year industry, manufacturers and retailers realize that POP offers impact, identification, and information for the consumer.

Marketers have long recognized the ability of packaging and POP to generate impulse buying, to support consumer price promotions, and to reinforce media communications. In recent years, though, packaging and POP have moved from being a companion marketing tool to a primary focus. Consumers make buying decisions in the store, brand loyalty is on the decline, and media advertising is losing effectiveness.

Point-of-Purchase Display

The very first POP display was a cigar-store Indian who held cigars in his hand. The first was created by tobacco companies in 1850 as a promotional device to keep the idea of cigar smoking planted in the mind of the consumer. Prominently placed at the

Advice from...
Linda Weeks, *Graphic Designer, Weeks Works*

Weeks created this lipstick display in three different sizes, making it easy for the client to accommodate different retailers' space requirements.

There are many design concerns when you're creating a POP display. First, you need to establish a sense of product and display coherence. The same colors, logos, type styles, illustration style, and "brand attitude" have to be instantly apparent on the display. It is very important that color is an exact match. Many of the companies that I work for have spec books that list the Pantone colors for logos, text, and trademarked items.

Second, you need to have a sturdy yet cost-effective display. If the display is meant to last for a two-month promotion, the material should last for two months of hard use. If it is a freestanding display, it has to be able to withstand bumps and shopping cart collisions for two months without disintegrating. It does not need to be as stable as a permanent display, and it should cost considerably less. Most of the displays for promotional or counter-top use are made of heavy, corrugated cardboard, and sometimes reinforced with lumber.

Determine the use your client has for the display. Can it go on a counter, or does it need to be freestanding? What goals should it achieve? Should it inform? Promote impulse buying? Offer free samples? Look at the print ads, media advertising, and other collateral material to get a feel for the colors and style of design they use. Get color swatches, and any logos on disk. Be certain the logos can be enlarged to the size necessary for the display.

entrance (the point of purchase) to a tobacconist, the consumer was "pitched" every time he passed by. The cigar-store Indian was a huge success, proving once again that a strong visual is vastly more important than a clever headline.

The way people shop today makes POP very important to manufacturers; we are in a hurry, want decisions to our purchasing questions instantly, don't have time to wait for a sales person, and usually make the decision to purchase a product while we are in a store, rather than coming in to the store already knowing what we are going to purchase. POP displays act as a silent, instantly accessible salesperson to quickly close a sale with all the facts necessary to influence purchasing decisions. An attractive display with an easily visible price and short, cogent information-bearing text is the hallmark of good POP design.

TYPES OF POP

POP displays range from small chewing gum racks at the checkout aisle to large electronic, interactive, freestanding kiosks for anything from light bulbs to cosmetics. POP is frequently used to promote short-term specials; cosmetics, which have seasonal changeover, rely heavily on this type of display. Sale items and special "limited time" offers of select merchandise also use POP. Another type of POP display, the "bin," is a large freestanding container, generally with a banner to grab the consumer's attention.

The easiest way to recognize POP is to take a walk through a large department store. You might see many of the following types:

- Premium display:
  These offer a special promotion to the consumer, usually in the form of a send-away premium. They usually display samples of the product and a form to mail in.

- Shelf extenders and shelf dividers:
  These are permanent trays used to arrange the product. They are fastened or clamped to the shelf and sometimes project from it.

- Counter display:
  These are self-service units in varying sizes; usually promotional displays that are placed on a counter.

- Gravity-fed displays:
  These are one of the oldest display systems, often used for small items. They can be hung on walls or stand on counters.

- Rotating displays:
  Designed to insure a permanent place in the store, and can be restocked with the merchandise; used primarily for items such as sun glasses, key chains, earrings, and other lightweight items.

No matter which type of POP is used, they are all created to be a "deal-closer." They help the consumer decide to buy the product by attractively displaying it, or by offering some additional information such as an amazing low price or a mail-in rebate. Any display which interactively engages the consumer, like a cosmetic display with samples or a spark plug tester, is sure to make a sale faster than a product that sits passively on the shelf. At the point of purchase, interest in the product can be turned immediately into action — a sale.

Packaging

Packaging follows the same line of reasoning as POP display. With hundreds of products available in even smaller retail outlets, what leads the consumer to buy one brand instead of another? The goal of packaging design is to create an attractive, inviting, and enticing piece which says "buy me!"

Packaging, like POP display, plays a major role in a consumer's decision to buy a product, which is why manufacturers spend billions of dollars in this market. Packaging is an extension of corporate identity, since it is the actual box (or bag or wrapper) you are likely to recognize. You may not remember the name of the cereal you really like, or what the logotype looks like, but you know it has a red box with a toucan on it. When you go to the store you can easily find that cereal you want because the package concept is branded in your mind.

As evidence that companies spend so much money on packaging, look for the generic or store brand of the same kind of cereal. Fruity Os don't taste a bit different from Fruit Loops, and they probably come close to the exact same nutritional content and ingredients. The store brand is usually much cheaper, since it's not in an elaborate box or bag — it may be in a simple clear bag that just says "Fruity Os." But (if you have some time) watch for a while and see how many people buy the recognized brand instead of the cheaper generic. Again, this is because the package and identity is branded in the consumer's mind.

When sales for a particular product drop off, the manufacturer often launches a "new-and-improved" product. And you can bet that the new product will involve a new packaging concept. More often than not, the only thing new about the improved version is

courtesy Impress Communications

Several examples of packaging. The boxes were designed to both ship and display the candy bars. The bottom image shows how packaging is printed — the flat printed sheet is scored so that it can be easily folded and assembled later.

the packaging; trends and consumer attitudes change over time, so manufacturers frequently revisit their packaging to stay current.

SPECIAL DESIGN CONCERNS FOR PACKAGING

Design for packaging can be one of the most difficult fields of graphic design. While other areas have certain conventions you should be aware of, packaging has very specific rules that have to be followed. For example, anything sold in a retail market almost always has to have a bar code (UPC symbol). These black-and-white bars could be a stumbling block depending on the look you want, but they still have to be there, so you need to design around it.

Packaging design for food has several requirements. In addition to the bar code, you also have to pay attention to Food and Drug Administration (FDA) requirements for nutritional content, list of ingredients, and any health warnings that need to appear on the package. Certain information has to be on food packaging, sometimes in very specific fonts and sizes; again, you have to design around these constraints.

In addition to these required elements, there are practical considerations to packaging design. What kind of product will go in the package? The physical matter of the package may need to withstand certain caustic substances (for cleansers or any other chemical-based product). If you're designing a package for frozen food, the material has to withstand very cold temperatures for a long period of time. Packages for produce have to be water resistent, or at least not disintegrate when wet. This is only a brief list; the important thing to remember is that you should learn about what you're packaging before you get too involved in the design concept.

SPECIAL MARKET SEGMENT — MUSIC INDUSTRY DESIGN

If you have a passion for music, you may have a niche in this market. It's small, hard to break into, and fiercely competitive (especially for larger recording labels), but music industry design is a great opportunity to combine a love of music and your design ability. As with any other field of graphic design, those who design for the music industry tend to work within a particular genre that matches their illustration style and interest.

Designing for the music industry requires a keen sense of a band's target market. You should have a working knowledge of the visual symbols, cues, and even typography that are popular in the genre of music you're designing for. Obviously, the visuals you would use for a folk artist would not attract rap listeners, and art for a rap artist probably wouldn't be popular with fans of classical music. Every music genre has its own look, and that look is a very important part of selling the music. Take frequent trips to record stores and subscribe to music magazines. Try to keep up with what's current in the music industry.

Tommy Gunn is a club band with a bluesy city sound. The gangster-type disco shark character visually sums up their sound.

Advice from...

Lorna Hernandez, *Creative Director, Paradox Creative Services*

When you design for the music industry, you have to really understand and love the music you're designing for. The band's unique attitude has to be expressed visually, so you have to be able to "get inside the sound" to portray the essence in a visual way. You can't do that very well if you don't like the music.

Musicians are artists, so they usually have a definite idea about what they want on their CD cover and the promotional material. I let them tell me their ideas, and I translate that into visual language.

If you want to break into this field, find a local band whose sound you love, and approach them with the idea of creating a package for them. You need a few different promotional packages in your design portfolio before you can approach recording or music promotion companies, and this gives you a trial run. This industry works by word of mouth — if you did a good job, other local bands will be calling you.

The CD cover is by far the most important piece of design for any band, but there are many graphic-design projects needed to promote a recording artist. The promotional package for a band or a musical artist contains a collection of items that are used to introduce the music to clubs, radio stations, and music stores. The package usually includes a press kit, which is a folder containing the CD, artist's bio and photograph, song list, and promotional material. The package might also include banners, flyers, t-shirts, bumper stickers, and other inexpensive promotional items.

CHAPTER 16

Advertising Design

If art struggles to create images of eternity, ads settle for what's happening right now. Advertising is the big-print edition of the Rosetta Stone, modern cave art in strobe lights.

JAMES B. TWITCHELL, *TWENTY ADS THAT SHOOK THE WORLD*

Advertising is, like graphic design, a very broad industry. Advertising takes many forms — from the 2-in. black-and-white classified ad in the back of a newspaper to a subtle sponsorship banner at the local little league field to the multimillion dollar 30-second spot aired during the Super Bowl — it's all advertising. Each of these forms serves the same purpose, which is to sell something.

There are many different advertising media: television, radio, newspapers, magazines, direct mail, banners, billboards, posters, the Internet, point-of-purchase, the list could go on. Advertising incorporates all of the ideas we've discussed in this book. The many available media allow (and in some cases require) you to develop a concept that works in print, on television, on the Internet, and over the radio, which makes good brainstorming essential. Advertising design stresses the importance of project unity — an advertisement is usually a part of a campaign, not an isolated incident. Like any single design project that needs unity throughout the piece, an ad campaign should also have some unifying theme, element, or message.

We've mentioned that logos and corporate identity need to be versatile; different advertising media are the primary reason. A company's logo, depending on the advertising budget, may be reproduced in a small Yellow Pages or classified newspaper ad, or as a full-color direct mail piece, or in a television commercial, or on a 12-ft. billboard. The logo needs to be readable at all these sizes, for all these media.

We've discussed, in various parts of this book, the importance of knowing your target market and understanding what motivates people to do certain things. Advertising design, perhaps more than any other field in the graphic design industry, relies heavily on these two elements.

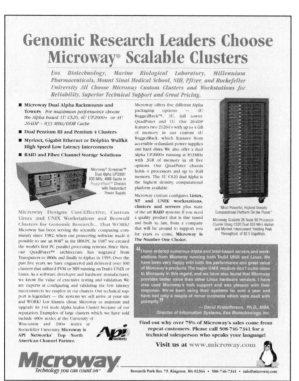

Depending on the target market, some advertisers choose to create a mock editorial page. This ad for Microway Inc. uses the same elements that you would find in an magazine article: headline, subheadline, body copy, images and captions, and footer.

This technique can be very successful in scientific and technical markets. The reader may be halfway through the page before realizing that it is an ad instead of an article.

Keep in mind that subscribers to scientific and technical magazines are more likely to actually read the pages cover-to-cover. Consumer and mass-market magazine subscribers generally flip through, glance at the pictures, and read one or two articles. Editorial-style ads would not be as effective for the general audience.

So What's It All About, Anyway?

Advertising is *persuasion*. It intends to reshape the way the consumer thinks, acts, and (more specifically) buys. The main goal of advertising is to place a product or service in the consumer mind. Companies spend billions of dollars every year to make sure you remember the product they sell. The most effective advertising is the kind which cements a product as the first thing we think of in any particular category. What comes to mind when you think of:

1. Rental cars?
2. Pizza delivery?
3. Computers?
4. Fast food?

Now consider these slogans:

1. "We'll pick you up."
2. "Pizza delivered to your door in 30 minutes or less. Guaranteed."
3. "Think different."
4. "Two all beef patties, special sauce, lettuce, cheese, pickles, onions on a sesame-seed bun."

The companies mentioned are, in order:
1. Enterprise Rent-a-Car; 2. Domino's Pizza; 3. Apple Computer; 4. McDonalds

If you've ever watched television, driven in a major city, or been in any airport in the U.S., you probably recognize at least two of these. (The answers appear at the bottom of these pages.) Were you able to pick the correct companies from just the category list? Did the slogans help? Most of us know these slogans because we see and hear them every day.

Now for a second test. Can you fill in the blank?

> Every day
>
> We do our part
>
> To make your face
>
> A work of art.

If you lived in the 1950s, you'd probably recognize this one quickly. The company had many similar slogans — short poems (since rhymes are easier to remember) with one line on each of a series of roadside signs. The advertising strategy was so popular that the memory lives on today in political campaigns, public service announcements, and other public interest markets.

Know Your Market

Recall from chapter 3, Abstraction, Symbolism, and Visual Metaphor, Maslow's hierarchy of human needs. Since advertising so heavily relies on these elements, they do bear repeating:

1. Survival (sex is associated with racial survival)

2. Security (personal and family safety)

3. Community (social and peer approval)

Successful advertising design is intended to sell something. Depending on your target market, either of these concerns may take highest priority. For example, if your target is 14 to 19-year-olds, you might assume that community takes precedence over security since security is usually not yet a concern at that age. If your audience is the 30 to 45-year-old single working-mother group, you can bet that security will be a prime concern. A thorough knowledge of your target market will greatly increase the effectiveness of your ad. Knowing what you are trying to sell and to whom you are trying to sell it is the most important key to advertising design.

Advice from...
Scott Reynolds, *Creative Director, Reynolds Roberts Creative Advertising and Graphic Design.*

It is very natural to think of the total ad when designing. When I think of the headline, I think not only of the words themselves, but also of the typeface I'm going to use and the kind of balance that would best reinforce the concept of the ad. I think of the headline as a verbal, conceptual element, as well as its role as a graphic design element — it's a part of the whole ad.

This ad, created for the Grand Palms Gold and Country Club by Roberts Reynolds Creative Group, is a lifestyle ad. The client is trying to sell townhouses using the idea of romance. The ad has a very specific target market: the more mature couple, well off with no children living at home. The ad sells a luxurious country-club lifestyle to a very targeted group of homebuyers. I used a variety of design principals to reinforce this concept.

The formal balance subconsciously reinforces the idea of traditional values, conservativeness, trustworthiness, and dignity. The typeface chosen for the headline also reinforces the notion that there was nothing trendy here, that this was no "faddish" temporarily fashionable community. The word "Renaissance" in the headline also conjures visual symbolism, since the Renaissance was the 12th century great revival of classical, Greek artistic aesthetics.

Promise, Amplify, Proof, Action

The very best advice about advertising comes from a senior creative director at D'Arcy Advertising. "It's simple," he says, "Just remember PAPA."

PAPA stands for promise, amplify, proof, action. The promise is the headline; it can be implied or clearly stated, and can be something as mundane as better mileage or as interesting as "getting the girl" (or guy). The promise might also be called the "hook."

Amplify your promise in the copy. Tell a little more about the product or service offered; keep it short for general markets. Longer amplifications work best for "serious" products, or ones for which facts and figures enhance the integrity of a company.

Proof is usually the visual part of an ad. People believe pictures. You can tell someone that he will have fun in his new truck, but no words are as convincing as a picture of the truck parked in a scenic locale or zipping through a forest.

Action refers to making it easy for a prospective customer to contact the advertiser. A phone number, email, or a Web address works fine. A nationally-known logo might also work as the call-to-action. For example, if a consumer sees a VW logo, they would be correct to assume that the product advertised is available at the local Volkswagen dealership.

The next time you flip through any magazine, examine the advertising. See if you can pick out the PAPA elements.

Developing a Full Campaign

It is important to devise a strategy that makes the best use of the various types of media. Careful consideration must be given to the advantages, both cost and marketability of newspaper ads; magazine ads; posters; brochures; billboards; leaflets and flyers; direct mail; and POP displays. The timeline is also important. Which will be launched first? The billboards, newspaper ads, direct mail pieces? How much time should pass between ads? As a good rule of thumb, allow three to six weeks before launching a new ad in the same campaign.

Special Market Opportunity — Writing Copy

We didn't include copywriter at the beginning of this section because it is not really a "graphic design" role. Most of the time, graphic design projects come with the copy already written, which means that you may never write a single sentence. Someone, though, had to write that text. If you enjoy writing and want to explore an area linked to graphic design, you may consider being a copywriter.

Writing ad copy is even more difficult than, say, writing a paper or letter. Ad copywriting is a special skill combining a firm grasp of language (including grammar and spelling) with the creative ability to make even the most mundane product sound attractive. There is a huge difference, to the consumer, between:

"We sell plants."

and

"Our garden and flower department welcomes
Spring just a bit early."

If you are a good writer, you should have no trouble finding work in the advertising field.

Advice from...
Scott Reynolds, *Creative Director, Reynolds Roberts Creative Advertising and Graphic Design.*

When I take on a new project, I first go on a fact-finding mission. I question the client and find out what their objectives are. Do they want to sell a specific car? Or do they want to develop an institutional ad that promotes the corporate identity?

Next, I find out how many colors the client wants to use, and what size the ad will be. What is the project budget? Who is the target market? I ask the client if they have a list of features or selling points, colors the product comes in, or any specific items they want the copy to include. I also ask the timeline and deadlines. I don't encourage clients to do my job, so I don't get much creative input from them. They hired me for my expertise, and they trust me to produce creative, interesting, effective ads. I do encourage them to keep me as informed as possible about objectives and selling points.

I develop three ads that would each work for the advertising objectives and within the specific job parameters. With the computer it is just as easy to do clean work as it is to do rough. I do everything on the computer, only the color proof is hard. The text may need a little tweaking, or some other minor change, but the ads are essentially done when I present them to the client. Usually clients like more than one, and occasionally they buy all three ads. It works out well for everyone.

Breaking into the Market

Look at what professional designers admire. Every year most of the magazines and trade organizations publish design annuals, which are judged by experts in the industry and highlight the best and brightest of the year. Read design magazines frequently, and try to keep up on current styles and trends. Study layouts and type treatments in these periodicals, and in general interest publications. Look at everything you see with an eye toward the design — the layout, the type choices, and the content. Subscribe to (and read) advertising industry magazines like *Advertising Age*, *Brandweek*, and *Adweek*.

Hold a Super Bowl party next year. Even if you have no interest in football, this is considered the end-all of prime advertising space. New campaigns are launched, new products and services introduced, and new trends are created during the Super Bowl commercials.

Go to the book store or library and find a copy of *Twenty Ads that Shook the World* by James B. Twitchell (Crown Publishers, 2000). The book provides a fascinating look at the techniques used by 20 of the most memorable advertising campaigns.

CHAPTER 17

Web Design and Multimedia

Another unsettling element in modern art is that common symptom of immaturity, the dread of doing something that has been done before.

—EDITH WHARTON

Designing for the Web

Only five years ago, the Internet was a foreign entity, primarily the realm of scientists, scholars, and the government. Now you don't even need to own a computer to access to the Internet — Web TV, e-machines, and independent Internet browsers are becoming so popular that you can surf the Web without having to buy an expensive computer system. It seems that practically everyone has email, if not their own Web site… can you think of a product or company that *doesn't* have a "dot com" tacked to its end?

As the Internet became more accessible and more affordable, it also became more popular. You can find just about anything you need or want on the Web. From Aunt Betty's famous brownie recipe to instant automobile insurance coverage to the vital statistics of your favorite celebrity, it's all out there.

The early stages of Web design were strictly limited to the world of computer programmers. HTML, (Hypertext Markup Language) is a computer language just as Basic, Pascal, C, and Cobol are languages. To "design" a Web page, you had to know the coding language, and be able to write hundreds (or even thousands) of lines of code to create even one page. Once the code was written, you uploaded it to a server and hoped that everything looked the way you wanted it to. More often than not you had to go back into your code and figure out what errors were causing what problems, fix them, and try it again until it worked.

This workflow gave Web design three important characteristics:

1. Early Web sites focused on information rather than appearance;

2. It was very expensive for people who wanted a website;

3. It was very lucrative for anyone who knew how to build a Web site.

As you probably know, times have changed. Software manufacturers developed new applications to visually create a Web site, so that you don't have to know HTML to build a functioning Web site. In fact, freeware and inexpensive consumer-based programs make it so easy to build a Web page that practically anyone can do it. This too has its drawbacks though.

Web design and multimedia are perhaps the best illustrations of the phrase "Just because you can doesn't mean you should." Just because you *can* put one line of type on each page, with thousands of little links to other pages on your site, doesn't mean you *should*. Just because you *can* use 24-pt flashing pink type doesn't mean you *should*. Just because you *can* use graphic-based software to do virtually anything, there are still conventions that you should pay attention to.

Once of the biggest problems with amateur Web sites is a complete lack of organization, which makes the site practically unnavigable. When you begin a Web design project, start by drawing a flowchart of all the elements you will eventually be including.

Site unity is important. Notice that each page in this site maintains a similar look and feel. The fourth image offers a thorough site map so that the user can easily navigate to any particular piece of information.

Advice from...
Seth Goldstein, *Director of Interactive Media Development, Fusive.*

"People say that the first 10 years of the Web were the era for the scientist. The sharing of information. The second 10 years is the era of marketing. But is that what people really want? All the animation, Flash files, flashing rollovers, and in-your-face-graphics? With the advent of wireless technology, we may see web design revert to content. The Web is *not* art, it is publishing and communication. The main criteria should always be usability.

"A large part of designing for the Web is learning what *not* to do. For instance, it's a bad idea to use gradients. They weigh a lot, take a long time to load, and usually look banded. Full-page illustrations are cumbersome, take way too long to load, and are never worth the wait. Tasteful, *restrained* use of animations is key. Stay away from clip-art, we have grown up. Avoid over-designing, and know when to stop. It is easy to become distracted from good design by the latest flashy little animations. They are not good design, they are decoration.

"A Web site is open-ended, it is not like a published brochure or an oil painting; when you design a Web site, keep in mind that it should be simple to update. Design the page so that it is easy to replace or swap-out information, rather than having to redesign the whole page when information changes. Good design should work for you."

Determine, before you create a single button or scan a single picture, what information goes where and how to present that information in a reasonably logical order. Once you've created this flowchart, you've got the solid foundation for your *site map*. That map helps you to unclutter the jumble of elements necessary for even the most straightforward site.

Web design, in essence, is just another kind of publication — you still should use the basic design principles, even though the presentation of is different. Maintain a consistent look and feel throughout your entire site. Use the same font size and style for different kinds of headlines, captions, and body text. Select a color scheme that you'll use for every page on the entire site. If you have a "Back" button on one page, use that same button every time a "Back" function is necessary. Just as you wouldn't design every page in a book to look differently, your Web site should carry a unified design from page-to-page.

When you're building the individual pages of a Web site, make sure you include navigation buttons that allow the user to easily jump from point A to point B, and back again. Web design, by its supposedly instantaneous nature, requires ease of use. If the person can't find the information they want in a few seconds or less, or if they get lost in your site and can't get back to the information they originally wanted, they'll simply go to the next site on the list.

What You See May Not Be What You Get

Just as print design has certain technical requirements, so does designing for the Web. Print design has a quality control department, preflighting or prepress, to make sure the technical aspects are correct. Web design, however, usually starts and ends with the designer. In some larger web design companies, or for more complex commerce sites, you will pass off your designs to a programmer to implement the site. But the programmers still can't program around technically impossible design. Be aware of these issues before you begin creating Web pages. You'll find that it's much easier to create you pages correctly at the beginning than it is to fix the problems later.

Even though PCs (formerly, and more appropriately, called IBM-compatible) by far dominate the personal-computer market, there are other kinds of computers in use today — Macintosh, UNIX, LINUX, and even Web TV, not to mention numerous other home-built variations. Each of these kinds of computers has its own operating system, which can vary greatly from one another. In addition to different operating systems, there are hundreds of different monitors available, each with different resolution, size, and color capabilities.

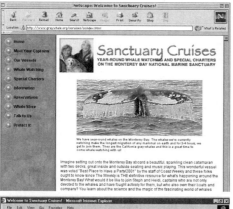

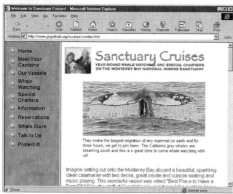

Now consider different Web browsers. Netscape Communicator and Internet Explorer are certainly the most used; but there are others, including AOL, CompuServe, and a host of smaller ones. Despite the almost universal use of HTML for Web design, there is not yet a standard version of the code. Netscape uses different HTML commands than Explorer to accomplish the same task. Though most of the code is the same, there are differences between browsers; each displays information differently.

Finally, you never can tell what a person wants to see. Just about any computer allows the user to set *preferences*, which include the standard (or *default*) font, type size, background color, and monitor resolution. Older people and people with poor eyesight tend to set default type at a much larger point size than what most designers would use. Unless you'll be visiting every one of your users to set their preferences, you have to keep these variations in mind when designing a Web site.

The same page as it looks on a Macintosh (top) and a PC (bottom). Notice that the fonts, which are designated Level 3 in HTML code, are much larger on the PC version than on the Mac.

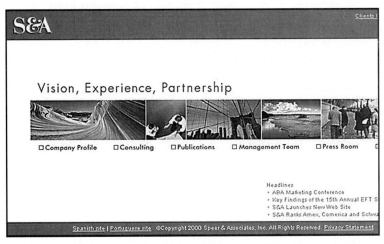

The point is that at least four different variables (platform, monitor, browser, and user preferences) can make your site vary greatly from user-to-user. Those variables multiply exponentially, making it nearly impossible to guarantee what your site will look like. Fortunately, the industry has created a few guides to smooth the path.

Typography separates a good site from a mediocre one. Everyone wants a "clean" site, uncluttered and clear with a lot of negative space — all the design rules still work. A case in point is this site developed for Speer & Associates (by Fusive). The generous use of negative space creates a visual "breath of fresh air": a far cry from web sites jammed with flashy animations and icons all over the place!

FONTS

Body copy for a Web site should be set in one of two fonts: serif or sans serif. The individual browser default will determine which font of that type to use. You can apply styling (italic, bold, underline, and so on.) to your fonts, and you can choose how large they will be (H1, H2, H3, and so on, getting progressively smaller).

If you absolutely need a font to appear a certain way, such as for a logo, page head, or other important element, create that item as an image. This is the only way to guarantee that a word always looks the same. This *does not* mean that you should create your entire page as one huge image, just so that you can control the font. When you create this kind of art, it works just like any other image — the files size increases and takes much longer to download. If you create your entire page as an image to control fonts, you may end up with huge files and extremely long download times.

COLORS

Because every monitor has different color capabilities and settings, the green you pick for headline type may not be the same as the green someone else sees when they go to your site. Most Web design programs have a built in color palette of 216 "Web-safe" colors, which you can reasonably assume will appear (closely) the same, regardless of where you view the site. If you use colors outside of that gamut, variations will occur and may or may not have very bad graphic results.

Advice from...
Seth Goldstein, *Director of Interactive Media Development, Fusive.*

It is possible to do everything a client wants and still have a site that fails in its purpose. Does the client want to win awards? Do they want to sell a product, or present information? Have a clear idea of the purpose first. Be a good listener. Remember that you're designing for the client and for the user, not for yourself. We develop a creative brief for every client to get the information we need.

At the beginning of a project, we hold collaborative meetings with clients to discuss what sites they like. We find out what tone and imagery they are already using in company logos, brochures, and annual reports. We work with their ad agency to get a style guide. We also ask the client to show us what they do not want. The main goal of these collaborations is to determine the purpose of the site, the target audience, the story, the tone and imagery, and the technical limitations.

Planning a Web site is a real team effort. For some reason everyone in a company, from the marketing department to senior vice presidents, always seem to have a pet idea to include about a company's Web site design. We take all the information, sift through everyone's input, and design a site that works. Stay on track with your client. Set reasonable expectations, put your objectives in writing, and be clear right from the start.

MONITOR SIZE

One important point is to think in terms of pixels instead of inches, because monitor resolution doesn't work in terms of inches. Web design conventions specify that sites should be confined to 480 pixels wide. According to this rule, you are safe to assume that everyone viewing your site will have at least a 14-in. monitor, which will fit 480 pixels across the screen. In fact, some design groups have proposed to set the standard page width at 780 pixels, or a 17-in. monitor.

CAVEAT: 14-in. monitors may seem small, especially if you're doing design work. But not everyone in the world has a 14- or 17-in. monitor, including anyone with a laptop. If you design a page larger than someone's monitor, they will have to scroll left and right to view the whole page — a web design *faux pas*. For some reason people don't really mind scrolling up and down, but left to right usually annoys people, which means they'll move on to the next site. We don't really know why this is true, it just is.

FILE SIZE AND DOWNLOAD TIME

Images and artwork take longer to download than text pages. When you're preparing images for a Web site, keep a close eye on the file size. If your files are too large, they'll take longer to download. Not everyone has a high-speed DSL or cable modem connection; many still rely on a standard dial-up modem, possibly still as low as 14.4 kbps. Larger files could take *hours* to view with a slow connection, and you can almost guarantee that the person will simply cancel your site and move on to the next one. This doesn't mean that you shouldn't use images. But try to keep download times relatively short when building your site.

Multimedia Design

Multimedia can be defined as any combination of words, sounds, pictures, and movies within a single user interface. Examples of multimedia include:

- An electronic slide presentation

- A CD-ROM encyclopedia

- A bridal registry kiosk in your local department store

Depending on your project, multimedia design follows many of the same principles as Web design.

PRESENTATIONS

Perhaps the most common type of multimedia design, electronic "slide shows," are often created to enhance a speaker's presentation. This type of multimedia project is frequently used for business and educational presentations, and is usually reliant on some type of software (such as PowerPoint).

A multimedia designer was hired to re-create a presentation for a Fortune 500 company; he created an attractive template which used consistent fonts and backgrounds throughout the presentation, incorporated sound and a short video clip, and even edited the text for proper grammar (which was above-and-beyond the scope of his responsibility). The company's CEO delivered the "new-and-improved" presentation to a large audience at a stockholder meeting. The designer asked for the CEO's feedback; after admitting that the presentation was the best the company had ever given, the CEO added, "But I really like the way the words used to fly onto the screen."

It bears repeating... just because you can, doesn't mean you should. Sadly, software has provided the ability to do just about anything — even if it is entirely inappropriate. Presentation design is afflicted by the same illness as Web design: virtually anyone can create a slide show, even if that person has no formal training in design principles. If you are designing a multimedia presentation, there are several rules to remember:

- Text, graphics, sound, and other elements should be incorporated to enhance what the speaker is saying.

- Avoid using graphics which would distract the audience's attention from the speaker's presentation (such as flying type.)

- Choose and place graphics carefully, and with some logical reason; avoid the random use of "word art" to "spice up" a piece that has no appropriate graphic.

- Use a consistent template throughout the presentation. The project should have a unifying color, background, and/or font scheme.

and finally...

- Do not try to display the entire verbal presentation on the slides.

As a general rule, you will not be responsible for creating the *content* of the visual presentation; that is usually provided by the speaker. But if at all possible, work with the content provider to develop an effective visual presentation that provides *additional value* to the audience, instead of simply repeating what the speaker will say.

INTERACTIVE CD-ROMS

If you wanted to buy the entire *Encyclopaedia Britannica*, you have two options: the 32-volume printed set for $1,300 or the CD-ROM interactive "deluxe" edition for approximately $50. Unless you love books, run a library, or just like getting heavy things in the mail, you can guess which version most people are likely to order.

Many multimedia CDs use a browser-like interface. The information on the CD is written into an HTML document; the opening screen looks like a Web page, possibly with a table-of-contents frame and a main window, and accessible with Netscape or Internet Explorer. Because it has the same look and feel, this kind of multimedia document is governed by virtually the same rules as web design.

Other multimedia CD-ROMs do not rely on browser capabilities. Instead, they are interactive software programs which either run directly from the CD, or require the user to install files to the hard drive. This type of multimedia application requires more intensive programming knowledge; a designer might partner with a computer programmer to develop an attractive-and-still-functional user interface. Though more programming intensive, this kind of design follows the *same set of rules* as any other Web or multimedia project:

- Your color scheme should stay within the 216 "Web-safe" color palette.

- For a browser-based multimedia CD, fonts must either be included on the CD with directions for the user to install, or should follow the serif/sans serif/default font structure; if the product is self-contained software, you are not constrained to only the user's system fonts.

- Keep standard monitor size in mind. Not everyone has a 21-in. monitor; if the target audience for your product is the general public, assume that many people will be using a 14-in. monitor.

- The interface should be intuitive and user friendly. If you place the navigation bar at the top of one screen, keep it there for all screens. Don't change the order of navigation buttons on different pages. Make information easily searchable.

- The main goal of most interactive multimedia is to present information. If you are creating an interactive directory, for example, people need to be able to quickly find and read the information they are looking for.

Since your product will be on a CD and not moving across the Internet, you are not as limited by file size. However, keep in mind that larger files still take more processing time. People with older or slower systems may not appreciate many large graphics files on every page.

INTERACTIVE KIOSKS

This is usually another partnering opportunity with a computer programmer. You will not need to write the code that makes the machine work; you create the look and feel of the kiosk, which is then coded by professional programmers. If you are hired to design an interactive kiosk, such as you might find in a mall, department store, or other retail outlet, you have very few constraints based on unknown variables. You will (presumably) know what size the final viewing area will be, and you will know what the system is technically capable of doing.

When you create a kiosk design, consider where it will be placed. Will it be in an airport or other internationally travelled area? You may need to incorporate different language options into your design. Will it be in a quiet setting? If so, loud noises may not be the best approach. Will it be in an arcade, amusement park, or some other area with lots of background noise? Then sound may not be effective or even necessary.

Interactive kiosks are almost always used to help people find information; maps, directions, and directories are the most common uses. Because information is the primary goal, you have two of the same rules that apply to multimedia CDs:

- The interface should be intuitive and user friendly. If you place the navigation bar at the top of one screen, keep it there for all screens. Don't change the order of navigation buttons on different pages. Make information easily searchable.

- If your kiosk needs to be accessible to people who speak different languages, use graphics rather than text whenever possible. Icons are usually understood, even if they don't speak the language you design with.

- Again, the main goal of an interactive kiosk is to present information. If you are creating an interactive directory, for example, people need to be able to quickly find *and read* the information they are looking for.

Gallery

You learned in Section 1 how to generate and develop an effective design solution. Section 2 presented the tools you need to create your designs. Section 3 provided an overview of the graphic design marketplace, including the different job functions and fields of design available to you in your career.

The following gallery offers numerous color examples to illustrate the concepts and ideas we've presented throughout this book, from effective use of color symbolism to successful Web site design, from researching a concept for a book cover to developing a complete corporate identity package. These projects were created by artists and designers from around the U.S., and represent a cross-section of the graphic design marketplace:

- Publication Design
- Information Graphics
- Editorial Illustration
- Corporate Identity
- Advertising Design
- Point-of-Purchase Display and Packaging
- Web Design and Multimedia

GASP

Creative Director:
Robin McAllister

The GASP Report is an excellent example of using two colors to present a more interesting final product. This newsletter also provides a valuable example of successful layout design for a text-heavy publication. The graphic on the cover breaks up a large block of text, and the runaround clipping path adds variety to straight margins.

The callouts exaggerate the same style used for the article subheads, maintaining consistency throughout the entire publication while adding visual breaks to text-heavy pages.

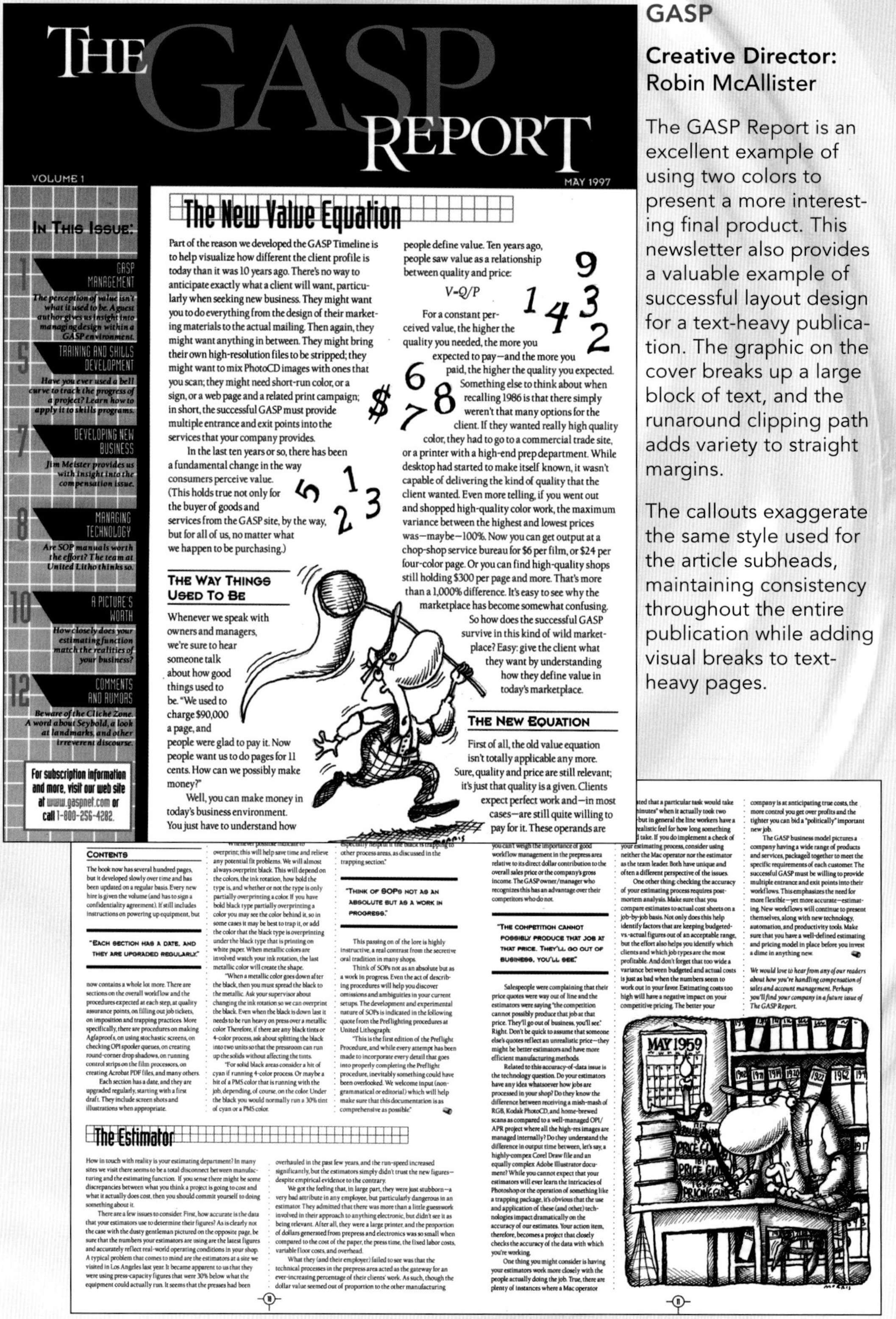

THE GASP REPORT

VOLUME 1   MAY 1997

IN THIS ISSUE:

1 — GASP MANAGEMENT
The perception of value isn't what it used to be. A guest author gives us insight into managing design within a GASP environment.

5 — TRAINING AND SKILLS DEVELOPMENT
Have you ever used a bell curve to track the progress of a project? Learn how to apply it to skills programs.

7 — DEVELOPING NEW BUSINESS
Jim Meister provides us with insight into the compensation issue.

8 — MANAGING TECHNOLOGY
Are SOP manuals worth the effort? The team at United Litho thinks so.

10 — A PICTURE'S WORTH
How closely does your estimating function match the realities of your business?

12 — COMMENTS AND RUMORS
Beware of the Cliche Zone. A word about Seybold, a look at landmarks, and other irreverent discourse.

For subscription information and more, visit our web site at **www.gaspnet.com** or call **1-800-256-4282.**

The New Value Equation

Part of the reason we developed the GASP Timeline is to help visualize how different the client profile is today than it was 10 years ago. There's no way to anticipate exactly what a client will want, particularly when seeking new business. They might want you to do everything from the design of their marketing materials to the actual mailing. Then again, they might want anything in between. They might bring their own high-resolution files to be stripped; they might want to mix PhotoCD images with ones that you scan; they might need short-run color, or a sign, or a web page and a related print campaign; in short, the successful GASP must provide multiple entrance and exit points into the services that your company provides.

In the last ten years or so, there has been a fundamental change in the way consumers perceive value. (This holds true not only for the buyer of goods and services from the GASP site, by the way, but for all of us, no matter what we happen to be purchasing.)

THE WAY THINGS USED TO BE

Whenever we speak with owners and managers, we're sure to hear someone talk about how good things used to be. "We used to charge $90,000 a page, and people were glad to pay it. Now people want us to do pages for 11 cents. How can we possibly make money?"

Well, you can make money in today's business environment. You just have to understand how

people define value. Ten years ago, people saw value as a relationship between quality and price:

$$V = Q/P$$

For a constant perceived value, the higher the quality you needed, the more you expected to pay—and the more you paid, the higher the quality you expected. Something else to think about when recalling 1986 is that there simply weren't that many options for the client. If they wanted really high quality color, they had to go to a commercial trade site, or a printer with a high-end prep department. While desktop had started to make itself known, it wasn't capable of delivering the kind of quality that the client wanted. Even more telling, if you went out and shopped high-quality color work, the maximum variance between the highest and lowest prices was—maybe—100%. Now you can get output at a chop-shop service bureau for $6 per film, or $24 per four-color page. Or you can find high-quality shops still holding $300 per page and more. That's more than a 1,000% difference. It's easy to see why the marketplace has become somewhat confusing. So how does the successful GASP survive in this kind of wild marketplace? Easy: give the client what they want by understanding how they define value in today's marketplace.

THE NEW EQUATION

First of all, the old value equation isn't totally applicable any more. Sure, quality and price are still relevant; it's just that quality is a given. Clients expect perfect work and—in most cases—are still quite willing to

---

Contents

The book now has several hundred pages, but it developed slowly over time and has been updated on a regular basis. Every new hire is given the volume (and has to sign a confidentiality agreement). It still includes instructions on powering up equipment, but

"EACH SECTION HAS A DATE, AND THEY ARE UPGRADED REGULARLY."

now contains a whole lot more. There are sections on the overall workflow and the procedures expected at each step, at quality assurance points, on filling out job tickets, on imposition and trapping practices. More specifically, there are procedures on making Agfaproofs, on using stochastic screens, on checking OPI spooler queues, on creating round-corner drop shadows, on running control strips on the film processors, on creating Acrobat PDF files, and many others.

Each section has a date, and they are upgraded regularly, starting with a first draft. They include screen shots and illustrations when appropriate.

whenever possible indicate to overprint; this will help save time and relieve any potential fit problems. We will almost always overprint black. This will depend on the colors, the ink rotation, how bold the type is, and whether or not the type is only partially overprinting a color. If you have bold black type partially overprinting a color you may see the color behind it, so in some cases it may be best to trap it, or add the color that the black type is overprinting under the black type that is printing on white paper. When metallic colors are involved watch your ink rotation, the last metallic color will create the shape.

"When a metallic color goes down after the black, then you must spread the black to the metallic. Ask your supervisor about changing the ink rotation so we can overprint the black. Even when the black is down last it needs to be run heavy on press over a metallic color. Therefore, if there are any black tints or 4-color process, ask about splitting the black into two units so that the pressroom can run up the solids without affecting the tints.

"For solid black areas consider a bit of cyan if running 4-color process. Or maybe a bit of a PMS color that is running with the job, depending, of course, on the color. Under the black you would normally run a 30% tint of cyan or a PMS color.

especially helpful is the black in trapping to other process areas, as discussed in the trapping section."

"THINK OF SOPs NOT AS AN ABSOLUTE BUT AS A WORK IN PROGRESS."

This passing on of the lore is highly instructive, a real contrast from the secretive oral tradition in many shops.

Think of SOPs not as an absolute but as a work in progress. Even the act of describing procedures will help you discover omissions and ambiguities in your current setups. The development and experimental nature of SOPs is indicated in the following quote from the Preflighting procedures at United Lithograph:

"This is the first edition of the Preflight Procedure, and while every attempt has been made to incorporate every detail that goes into properly completing the Preflight procedure, inevitably something could have been overlooked. We welcome input (nongrammatical or editorial) which will help make sure that this documentation is as comprehensive as possible"

The Estimator

How in touch with reality is your estimating department? In many sites we visit there seems to be a total disconnect between manufacturing and the estimating function. If you sense there might be some discrepancies between what you think a project is going to cost and what it actually does cost, then you should commit yourself to doing something about it.

There are a few issues to consider. First, how accurate is the data your estimators use to determine their figures? As is clearly not the case with the dusty gentleman pictured on the opposite page, be sure that the numbers your estimators are using are the latest figures and accurately reflect real-world operating conditions in your shop. A typical problem that comes to mind are the estimators at a site we visited in Los Angeles last year. It became apparent to us that they were using press-capacity figures that were 30% below what the equipment could actually run. It seems that the presses had been

overhauled in the past few years, and the run-speed increased significantly, but the estimators simply didn't trust the new figures—despite empirical evidence to the contrary.

We got the feeling that, in large part, they were just stubborn—a very bad attribute in any employee, but particularly dangerous in an estimator. They admitted that there was more than a little guesswork involved in their approach to anything electronic, but didn't see it as being relevant. After all, they were a large printer, and the proportion of dollars generated from prepress and electronics was so small when compared to the cost of the paper, the press time, the fixed labor costs, variable floor costs, and overhead.

What they (and their employer) failed to see was that the technical processes in the prepress area acted as the gateway for an ever-increasing percentage of their clients' work. As such, though the dollar value seemed out of proportion to the other manufacturing

you can't weigh the importance of good workflow management in the prepress area relative to its direct dollar contribution to the overall sales price or the company's gross income. The GASP owner/manager who recognizes this has an advantage over their competitors who do not.

"THE COMPETITION CANNOT POSSIBLY PRODUCE THAT JOB AT THAT PRICE. THEY'LL GO OUT OF BUSINESS, YOU'LL SEE."

Salespeople were complaining that their price quotes were way out of line and the estimators were saying "the competition cannot possibly produce that job at that price. They'll go out of business, you'll see." Right. Don't be quick to assume that someone else's quotes reflect an unrealistic price—they might be better estimators and have more efficient manufacturing methods.

Related to this accuracy-of-data issue is the technology question. Do your estimators have any idea whatsoever how jobs are processed in your shop? Do they know the difference between receiving a mish-mash of RGB, Kodak PhotoCD, and home-brewed scans as compared to a well-managed OPI/APR project where all the high-res images are managed internally? Do they understand the difference in output time between, let's say, a highly-complex Corel Draw file and an equally complex Adobe Illustrator document? While you cannot expect that your estimators will ever learn the intricacies of Photoshop or the operation of something like a trapping package, it's obvious that the use and application of these (and other) technologies impact dramatically on the accuracy of our estimates. Your action item, therefore, becomes a project that closely checks the accuracy of the data with which you're working.

One thing you might consider is having your estimators work more closely with the people actually doing the job. True, there are plenty of instances where a Mac operator

that a particular task would take minutes" when it actually took two but in general the line workers have a realistic feel for how long something will take. If you do implement a check of your estimating process, consider using neither the Mac operator nor the estimator as the team leader. Both have unique and often a different perspective of the issues.

One other thing: checking the accuracy of your estimating process requires postmortem analysis. Make sure that you compare estimates to actual cost sheets on a job-by-job basis. Not only does this help identify factors that are keeping budgeted-vs.-actual figures out of an acceptable range, but the effort also helps you identify which clients and which job types are the most profitable. And don't forget that too wide a variance between budgeted and actual costs is just as bad when the numbers seem to work out in your favor. Estimating costs too high will have a negative impact on your competitive pricing. The better your

company is at anticipating true costs, the more control you get over your profits and the tighter you can bid a "politically" important new job.

The GASP business model pictures a company having a wide range of products and services, packaged together to meet the specific requirements of each customer. The successful GASP must be willing to provide multiple entrance and exit points into their world lives. This emphasizes the need for more flexible—yet more accurate—estimating. New workflows will continue to present themselves, along with new technology, automation, and productivity tools. Make sure that you have a well-defined estimating and pricing model in place before you invest a dime in anything new.

We would love to hear from any of our readers about how you're handling compensation of sales and account management. Perhaps you'll find your company in a future issue of The GASP Report.

MAY 1959

ARTEMIS DESIGN GROUP

Creative Director: Chrissy David
Client: Justice House Publishing

The publisher wanted to recreate the look of the "dime novel" type of popular publication in the 1800s, which is when the story took place. David researched and found the style of typography from that period, drew the sketch for the cover art in the style of the 1800s and used an old map as a wraparound background. The final book and its separate elements are shown here.

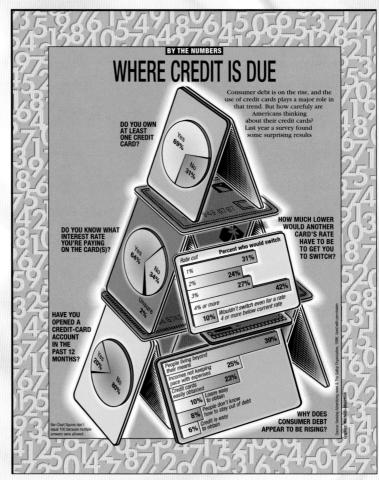

SCOTT MACNEILL

MacNeill and Macintosh
Client: Fidelity Investments

These two images exemplify several important quality-of-information graphics. MacNeill was contracted to create two full-page information graphics for *Stages* magazine. The client provided the statistics, and MacNeill used his (in his words) utilitarian style to create visually interesting, informative graphics. Since both images were part of the same article (notice the "By the Numbers" heading on each), MacNeill used a consistent background to enhance the project unity. Even if you don't read a single word in the article, you can quickly pick out the important statistics from MacNeill's images. These concepts for these images were created using traditional media: tissue, vellum, markers, and pencils; the final sketches were scanned and re-created digitally.

The most important factor in becoming an illustrator is to develop a style. Illustration aims to solve a problem visually; according to MacNeill, you should "develop a style that can successfully solve 99% of those problems. Your style, though, should constantly evolve, since new problems always come up. The process should be ongoing, never static.

"Freelance illustration has declined sharply in recent years, largely due to the availability of clip art. There are less problems with clip art, including no copyright issues and no temperamental illustrators. If you want to eventually work as an illustrator, start at a design firm and work illustration into your role at that agency. You'll be able to exercise your creative energy while still paying the bills; you can also use your time at an agency to really develop your style."

SNACK ATTACK

Enjoying three square meals a day used to be a nutritional standard to aspire to, but increasingly Americans are opting for fewer meals and more snacks. In the last 10 years the number of Americans who say they eat three meals a day with no between-meal snacks has dropped from 33% to 24%. The younger you are the more likely you are to eschew three squares a day in favor of chewing on a snack or two. Here are some more figures on Americans' on-the-run nutritional habits.

MAKE MINE A LITE
(Percent who say they favor the "light" version of given foods/beverages)

Milk 48%
Soft drinks 24%
Ice cream 20%
Cheese 18%
Salty snacks 17%

MOST POPULAR SNACKS
(in decreasing order)

Fresh fruit 1
Potato chips/salty snack 2
Cookies 3
Donuts 4
Candy 5
Danish/pastry 6
Crackers 7
Popcorn 8
Bagel 9
Yogurt/nuts (tie) 10

HOW OFTEN DO YOU SNACK AT WORK?

Not sure 7%
Almost every day 38%
Never 20%
14%
Occasionally 21%
Couple times a week

MOM's

WHO EATS HOW?
(Age Influences Meals vs. Snacks Behavior)

Three meals, no snacks
Three meals, plus snacks
Two meals, no snacks
Other
Two meals, plus snacks

Ages 18-29
16%
26%
15%
13%
31%

Ages 30-44
20%
23%
14%
15%
28%

Ages 45-59
27%
24%
9%
25%
15%

Ages 60+
35%
7%
26%
20%
12%

Source: Roper Starch Worldwide, 1996

Graphics: MacNeill+Macintosh

INFORMATION GRAPHICS

SCOTT MACNEILL

MacNeill and Macintosh
Client: Internet News

Editorial illustration, including magazine covers, is intended to tell a story without the need for text. Internet News, an Italian magazine, contracted MacNeill to create these two covers. Even if you don't read or speak Italian, the images give you an idea of the issue's theme.

Though many magazines prefer a photographic cover image, MacNeill was hired for this project because of his unique style of illustration. There has, he states, been a backlash against computer-generated art and photo collage work. "Photo collages are too realistic. They are too real, and people are uncomfortable with that." These images might easily have been created with photographic manipulation, but MacNeill's style leaves little room for the viewer to mistake reality.

Much of MacNeill's illustration work comes through referrals from current clients. His advice to the beginning illustrator is to "have a rock solid ego. If you come away from one of five jobs with a satisfied client, consider yourself lucky. Your goal is to make the client happy, so you need to be able to walk away from nasty comments and harsh criticism if you want to keep making a living."

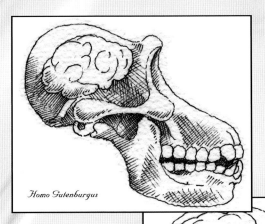

Homo Gutenburgus

DON MORRIS

Illustrator
Client: The Gasp Report

A series of related illustrations can often help the evolution of a story or article. These four images are appropriate examples of sequential editorial drawings. In these images, we see human evolution in a light-hearted progression that ends up with a mythical creature genetically adapted to life inside of a professional graphic arts environment. You may notice he has eye sockets all around his head, and a universal serial interace on the side of his skull. These physical features allow him to watch everything while being wired directly into the department's servers.

Illustrations like these are created specifically for the story they support; standard or "stock" art normally can't meet the requirements. This example, from *The Gasp Report*, was the result of a collaboration between the editors and Don Morris, Art Director of the *St. Petersburg Times* — one of the nation's leading daily newspapers. Each month, the editors would discuss the topic and determine what sort of illustrations they would need to support the story. The project was a monthly article called "A Picture's Worth," which took a humorous look at specific management concerns. The idea behind Digitalis was that normally evolved human beings weren't physically capable of managing a typical, hectic and demanding graphic arts business.

Homo Lithos

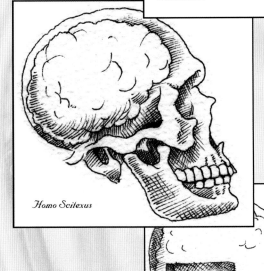

Homo Scitexus

Homo Directus v. digitalis

EDITORIAL ILLUSTRATION

IMPRESS COMMUNICATIONS

Graphic Designers: Michelle Franks, Robert Diaz, Ernestine Sun, Dennis Lagodimos
Art Director: Paul Marino, Vice President of Sales & Marketing

Corporate identity, as we discussed previously, encompasses much more than a logo and letterhead. Impress Communications created its own identity package (shown below) in the form of this presentation kit. The package includes a presentation folder; recent press releases; a services booklet that includes printing samples for everything from four-color to metallics to embossing; an equipment list; and premiums such as tablets, a mouse pad, CD-size calendar, branded water bottle, and a pen.

This package won high honors at the IAPHC's 2000 International Gallery of Superb Printing, including a Gold Award for superb craftsmanship in the design and production of the kit box; a Gold Award for superb craftsmanship in the design and production of the calendar; a Gold Award for superb craftsmanship in the design and production of the stationery package; and a Bronze Award for superb craftsmanship in the design and production of the presentation folder.

GALLERY OF GRAPHIC DESIGN

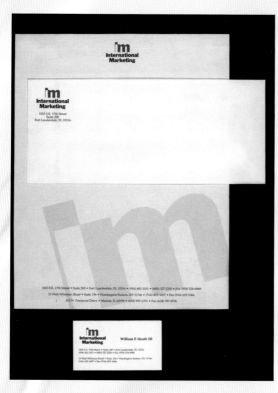

BING! DESIGN

Graphic Designer: Andy Bing
Client: International Marketing,
Products that Produce

This design for International Marketing plays on negative and positive space to create the logotype. Red makes the "IM" stand out from the rest of the logotype. Red and blue ink on white stock neatly ties American values to the international company. The "IM" graphic was also rendered as a percentage and screened across the letterhead, which lightens up a design that could have become staid.

REYNOLDS ROBERTS CREATIVE ADVERTISING AND GRAPHIC DESIGN

Creative Director: Scott Reynolds
Client: ExecJet

The small jet company needed a luxurious presentation package on a budget. The two-color job appears to be much more expensive than it really was to print. Reynolds used a screened image of clouds printed in the same ink color as the logo to lend depth and texture to the design. A rich brown ink was used, which carries all the attributes of traditional quality. The stationery is printed on a midweight, smooth ivory stock. Reynolds comments, a bit ruefully, "It is a sad truth for graphic designers, but the paper weight and texture a company uses for its stationery say more about a company than a brilliant logo design. People are acutely aware of quality in paper texture." So, he didn't scrimp on this important facet of corporate design. Because the company was working within a budget, Scott designed the accompanying brochure to fit in a #10 envelope, which requires only normal postage to send.

Creative Director: Scott Reynolds
Client: Ed Morse Chevrolet, Allen Morris

This ad was specifically designed to run in the Swimsuit Edition of *Sports Illustrated* magazine. The ad directs the viewer's eye first to the visual — the sexy red car, warm luscious light, and the handsome couple. The viewer's eye then moves to the headline, which is a visual and conceptual juxtaposition — the use of negative and positive type, and the opposite ideas of being able to "own" a "supermodel." The hairline box acts as a platform for the car to rest on, and concretely connects the illustration and text elements. The page curl is set at the extreme boundary of the live area of the page; even if the ad ran on the left-facing page of the magazine, the slogan would not be lost in the gutter.

Allen Morris, a commercial real estate management company, wanted an ad that related the idea that they had been around a long time and would be around and going strong in the future. This ad was intended for business magazines; every other commercial management ad in these publications shows a building, and has a headline saying "We manage this building, let us manage yours, too." Morris wanted an ad that sold the idea of stability without being hidebound. First, the asymmetrical balance is very stable, establishing a company "poised for the future." The reverse-type headline further reinforces this fresh idea.

Morris wanted a visual that represented the tradition of integrity: the eagle and all the symbolism it holds was a perfect choice. The client loved this stock image of a paper cutout eagle; they purchased the rights to use the image for one year in their market, which ensures that a competitor cannot use that image at the same time.

ARTEMIS DESIGN GROUP

Designer: Chrissy David
Client: Zippo, Bethesda Hospital

This two-page ad for Zippo is designed to look like a 1950s advertisement, from an era when every man owned a Zippo lighter. The ad is a promotion for a free booklet on cigars, which continues the same theme.

This brochure for Bethesda Hospital uses a combination of photographic and sketched imagery. During the research phase of this design project, David learned that the word *bethesda* means "Pool of Healing" in the Bible and in Jewish historical records. The imagery and the color choices use water to reinforce that symbolism.

Creative Director: Lorna Hernandez
Client: Freak the Jones, "Pass the Salt" and "OHM"
CDs and Promotional package

Freak the Jones has a funky, psychedelic rock sound. The band, based in Atlanta, has a very tongue-in-cheek sense of humor. Their input was that the tray card should be a collage of phenomena such as alien abduction, conspiracy theory, Elvis sightings, and Freak the Jones sightings. The "Freak" character is a stylized take on the lead singer/bass player, Buddha. This icon is featured on T-shirts and other promotional material. The CD title, "Pass the Salt," is based on the painting which is featured on the cover. The loose, asymmetrical balance and casual text treatment is appropriate for this irreverent band. Note that the band's name and song titles on the tray-card are the only very legible elements on an otherwise erratic, confusing collage.

This CD and promotional material continue the alien and Elvis sighting theme, which has become a hallmark of Freak the Jones promotional material. The tray card is again a collage of icons and graphical references gleaned from the lyrics themselves. The cover, which features lightning bolts emerging from a speaker, is the specific imagery requested by the group's lead singer. The CD title, "OHM," refers to the electrical measurement and also to the Buddhist chant OM. The band refers to the CD as an electronic prayer on the tray card, a musical OM. The promotional package consists of the folder, bio and photo, song list, backstage pass, bumper sticker, activity book, and whoopee cushion. The design and color choices throughout reflect the joyful, passionate, and casual attitude of the band.

WEEKS WORKS

Linda Weeks, Owner Graphic Designer
Client: Prestige Cosmetics

This display targets the teenage market. The design is fun, lively, energetic, and carefree. The vibrant teenage model, polka-dots, and bright colors reinforce the appeal to young girls. The visual elements are incorporated into a dynamic design, using repeating diagonal lines to keep the visual energy flowing, and thus reinforcing the energetic, young appeal. The credit-card shape and size of the product suggests freedom — not being encumbered by a purse for all you cosmetics. The best attention grabber, a free item, is highly visible.

The frosted acrylic banner display and pastel packaging reinforces the product's clean, fresh qualities. The leaf shape in the banner suggests "natural" products, the silver foil leaf "O" in the name reinforces the natural concept with a more modern twist. Icy, pastel colors for the packaging design reinforce the cool, clean qualities of the lotions and gels. The formal arrangement of products within the display speaks to the straightforward approach the company takes to beautiful skin: clean, toned, natural. Their traditional approach is reinforced and amplified by this formal, traditional balance.

POP AND PACKAGING DESIGN

WWW.DOGTECH.COM

Designed by
Doghouse Technologies, Inc.

Many Web sites suffer from "Information Overload" syndrome; these images clearly show how simplicity can be the key to good Web site design. Doghouse Technologies uses a simple and easy-to-read interface, all contained within one screen (no scrolling), to present their information. Intuitive links allow the user to find the desired information quickly.

WWW.A-NOVOBROADBAND.COM
WWW.FURNITUREESUPERSTORE.COM
WWW.ICCWEB.COM

Designed by Doghouse Technologies, Inc.

Additional Doghouse Technologies designs show the group's diverse capabilities. Their portfoilo ranges from basic informational sites (such as Novo Broadband, *www.a-novobroadband.com*) to online e-commerce sites (Furniture E Superstore, *furnitureesuperstore.com*) to complete online searchable databases (Internet Career Connection, *www.iccweb.com*). In each case, the sites are both attractive *and* functional.

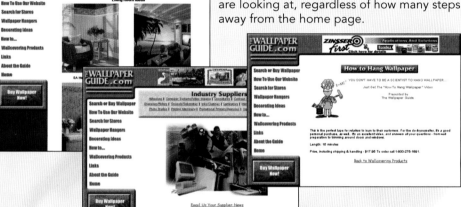

WWW.WALLPAPERGUIDE.COM

Designed by Doghouse Technologies, Inc.

This site is an excellent example of combining form and function into an attractive and informational Web site. The introductory screen (left) offers easy and intuitive navigation buttons and a scrolling information window, all presented within a format that requires no scrolling. Secondary pages offer everything from browsing wallpaper samples to decorating ideas to hints on how to hang wallpaper. Notice that each screen in the site maintains the same look and feel, so that users will know exactly what site they are looking at, regardless of how many steps away from the home page.

FUSIVE

Seth Goldstein, Director of Interactive Media Development
Client: Burger King Corporation

These two pages are from the Burger King Corporation's Web site during the Pokémon® The Movie 2000 promotion. The clean use of white space makes it easy to navigate the main page. Also notice that the layout is designed so it would be simple to update the site on a regular basis. The Pokémon page echoes the design from the main page in the placement of the navigational buttons along the Burger King trademark's circular path.

TM and © 2000 Burger King Brands, Inc.

ARTISTS WHO CONTRIBUTED WORK TO THIS BOOK:

Andy Bing
Owner, Bing! Design
www.bings.com

Chrissy David
Artemis Design Group
Ft. Lauderdale, Florida

Doghouse Technologies, Inc.
Brent and Allen Edger
www.dogtech.com

Liesel Donaldson
Graphic Designer
www.liesel.com

Marianne Frasco
Design Manager, Prentice Hall
Upper Saddle River, New Jersey

Ana Giraldo
Miami, Florida

Seth Goldstein
Director of Interactive Media Development,
Fusive.com
www.fusive.com

Lorna Hernandez
Creative Director, Paradox Creative Services
www.paradoxcreative.com

Impress Communications
Los Angeles, California
www.impress1.com

Scott MacNeill
MacNeill and Macintosh
macmac@dvic.com

Don Morris
Art Director, *St. Petersburg Times*
St. Petersburg, Florida

Scott Reynolds
Creative Director, Reynolds Roberts Creative
Advertising and Graphic Design
Pompano, Florida

Linda Weeks
Graphic Designer, Weeks Works
Pompano, Florida

A big thanks to all of the students from
the Art Institute of Ft. Lauderdale who
contributed their artwork to this book.

GALLERY OF GRAPHIC DESIGN

Glossary

Advertisement

A commercial space. Areas in newspapers and magazines which are contracted for the sole purpose of promotion of items such as a product, activity or event.

Art Director

An employee, often of an advertising agency, who supervises design creation.

Balance

The arrangement of shapes, illustrations and text on a page or within a publication.

Book

A compiled work of individual sheets or signatures, bound together as a unit. The most common form of mass written communication for novels, poetry, nonfiction, educational texts, and similar literary efforts.

Brainstorming

Developing a concept of a graphic design.

Catalog

A purpose-specific publication designed to advertise and sell goods and/or services, usually offered by a single company. They can be anything from a small pamphlet or brochure to a several hundred page book. Catalogs are typically printed on glossy paper to enhance the appearance of advertising products. Covers may be printed on a heavier stock to prevent ripping.

Color

Physiologically, a visual sensation produced in the brain when the eye views various wavelengths of the light. Color viewing is a highly-subjective experience that varies from individual to individual and instance to instance. In the graphic arts industry, lighting standards and color charts help ensure the accuracy of color reproduction.

Color Depth

Known also as "bit depth," color depth is defined as the number of colors that can be defined for each pixel on your monitor. Different monitors have different color depth, ranging from 1-bit to 24- or 32-bit (which can display millions of colors).

Color Gamut

The range of colors that can be formed by all possible combinations of the colorants of a particular color reproduction system.

Color Reproduction (Guide)

A printed image consisting of solid primary, secondary, three- and four-color, and tint areas. It is primarily used as a guide for color correction of the defects of the printing ink pigments and the color separation system. Most experts suggest that the guide be produced locally under regular plant production conditions.

Color Wheel

A circular tool used by graphic designers that shows the primary, secondary, and intermediate colors.

Complementary Color

Opposite colors on the color wheel. Complementary colors in a design can enhance and strengthen the appearance that the designer is trying to highlight.

Decorative Type

An alternate name for display or novelty type. One of the five classifications of type, it has no specific definitive features except that it is generally unsuitable for body copy; should be used in large sizes and minimally. An attention-getting type, almost always of unusual design.

Design

A partnership between creative thought and the elements that comprise the visual language.

Diecutting

The process of using sharp steel rules to make cuts in printed sheets for boxes, pop-up brochures and other specialized printing jobs.

Direct Mail

A form of advertising materials mailed directly to the potential customer; they are designed to stimulate direct readers' response to purchase, donation, enroll, subscribe, and so forth.

Editor

A person who selects words and visual elements such as photographs so they accomplish their communication goals within the space and budget allocated them.

Editorial Illustration

Differing from information graphics, since it is not intended to be an exact depiction of specific facts, editorial illustration works from the concepts presented in the text to enhance the information, or as a visual depiction of a story without any accompanying text.

Embossing

To impress paper into bas-relief by pressing it between special dies on a heavy-duty press. Special female dies are used with a male counter created by making ready with a special compound. The process of producing a printed raised (relief) image in paper (substrate).

Filter

In general black-and-white and color photography, a colored sheet of transparent material such as gelatin, acetate or glass, that is mounted in front of a camera or enlarger lens to emphasize, eliminate, or change the color or density of the entire scene or certain elements in the scene by absorbing specific colors or wavelengths. They may also be used to soften or otherwise alter image characteristics.

Foil Stamping (Foil Emboss)

A relief process used for the placement of metallic or pigmented colors onto a substrate using specially engraved or cut dies, heat, and pressure. Flat foiling transfers only the image. Foil stamping transfers the image and distresses the paper to give the foil additional depth and dimension.

Folding Dummy

A dummy signature or compiled product sample made of paper specified for the printing job. Used to illustrate imposition of pages on a press sheet.

Framing the Shot

A term used to ensure (usually in conjunction with a tripod) that the area chosen for a photograph will remain the same in every shot.

Framing the Subject

It is a good idea to use elements to lead the viewer's eyes into the picture. Use a tree limb, a doorway, a window frame, foliage, or similar elements to direct the viewer's attention to the subject. This technique also quickly establishes depth in the image, which is one of the powerful attributes of excellent photographic composition.

Graphic Design

The process of solving a problem visually.

Graphic Designer

A professional who conceives a design, plans how to produce it, and may coordinate production of a printed piece.

Greeking

(1) Body text that is made illegible when viewed at 12 points or below, for the purpose of speeding screen redraw or creating a rough layout. (2) Nonsensical character combinations and spaces used to simulate text in body copy blocks on roughs.

Grid

A layout template with defining guides for the margins, space between columns, and the space between a caption and an illustration. Also known as *master pages*.

High-traffic Design

Maps, menus, and similar kinds of work requiring paper that can stand up to a lot of abuse. Menus and maps need to be sturdy enough to last for more than one use, and have a certain degree of wet strength. Both of these types of work also need paper with a high level of folding endurance.

Hyphenation and Justification (H&J)

An algorithm that determines line endings and spacing, used by page layout programs. Sophisticated programs follow a standard dictionary or a special dictionary created by the user for unusual or field-specific terms, and allow adjustment of the H&J parameters.

Icons

Graphic symbols designed to convey information quickly in a stylized, abstracted manner.

Illustration

A general term for any photograph, drawing, diagram, or image that serves to enhance a printed piece. The term is commonly used to indicate drawings or diagrams to differentiate them from photographs.

Imposition

The final stage of the design process, directly before anything can be printed. The term refers to the arrangement of pages or elements on a printed sheet so that all elements will be in the correct position once folding, binding, and finishing processes are complete.

Information Graphics

Often abbreviated to "infographics," information graphics are created to display information in some visual manner other than text. Information graphics are generally used to visually represent complex statistics, numerical or scientific data, or some other item that benefits from a pictorial description.

Kerning

To mortise. (1) The process of using negative letter space between specific character combinations so that they appear closer together. Typesetting characters are positioned within an imaginary rectangle of a specific width value. Typographic kerning defines characters by their shape as well as their width by optically reducing the space between certain letter combinations and programming them into the typesetting system. Kerned letters are common in italic, script, and swash fonts.

Lamination

The process of placing a thin layer of transparent film on one or both sides of a printed sheet to provide protection, durability, and to give it a glossy finish.

Layout

The arrangement of visual elements on a page (or throughout the publication).

Layout Artist

A person who visualizes how the final printed product will look and makes the base layouts that the production workers will use to execute the design.

Leading (Line Spacing)

In modern typography, the distance from the baseline of a line of type to the baseline of the line above it; less frequently measured from ascender to ascender, expressed in points of hundredths of an inch. Also called film advance and line spacing.

Letter (Paper)

In North America, 8.5 × 11-in. sheets. In Europe, A4 sheets.

Line (Emotional Content)

The emotional response that we associate with linear movement.

Lines

Used in a design to denote a boundary.

Line Spacing

A term used for leading in photo-typesetting. Measured in points from one baseline to the next baseline. Related Term: *Leading*.

Logo

A corporate or organizational identifier.

Multimedia

Any combination of words, sounds, pictures, and movies within a single user interface.

Packaging

(1) Printing papers made for specific packaging applications, such as food, whose papers must meet government sanitary standards.

Pantone Matching System (PMS)

The most commonly used ink mixing and color reference formula. It consists of a dozen or so carefully formulated colors which, when mixed in the proportions indicated on a reference chart, produce several thousand predetermined colors for spot reproduction.

PAPA

An advertising acronym that stands for "promise," "amplify," "proof," "action." The promise is the headline; it can be implied or clearly stated. The promise might also be called the "hook." Amplify your promise in the copy. Proof is usually the visual part of an ad. Action refers to making it easy for a prospective customer to contact the advertiser.

Paper

A substrate for printing and writing that is made of cellulose fibers from trees and/or other plants, and which are sometimes combined with artificial fibers.

Paper Weight

Refers to the physical weight of 500 sheets at the paper's basic sheet size. If the paper mill cuts paper to the basic size of 35 × 38-in., then 500 of those sheets provide the paper weight: 20 lb., 80 lb., 100 lb., and so on.

Periodical

A publication such as a magazine or newspaper that is published at regular intervals.

Point-of-Purchase Display

A box or rack, sometimes made of sturdy cardboard, that displays merchandise near the location of the sales transaction.

Postcards

These projects always use paper thick enough to withstand mailing, usually 100+ lb. card stock (hence, the name). Postcards are usually higher-quality paper than reply cards. Related Term: *Reply Cards*.

Prepress

A term to describe all printing operations prior to presswork, including design and layout, typesetting, computer applications of full page composition, graphic arts photography, color separation, image assembly, color proofing and platemaking.

Promotional Material

All of the media and/or other merchandise designed to publicize and sell a product.

Proof

(1) A prototype of the printed job; a reasonably accurate representation of how a printed job is intended to look. It can be made photomechanically from plates (a press proof), photochemically from film and dyes, or digitally from electronic data. Prepress proofs serve as samples for the customer and guides for the press operators. Press proofs are approved by the customer and/or plant supervisor before the actual pressrun.

Proofreader

The person who carefully reads and reviews typeset copy for errors, spelling, spacing, positioning, and so forth.

Reply Cards

Like postcards, these projects use paper thick enough to withstand mailing, usually 100+ lb. card stock (hence, the name). Related Term: *Postcards*.

Rough

A full-size rendition of a design, in many cases incorporating elements from several different thumbnails.

Rule of Thirds

A simple rule of composition for photography: If a photograph is divided into thirds with horizontal and vertical lines, the intersection of these lines mark the position for compelling photographic composition.

Sans Serif

Literally, "without serifs." One of the five type classifications; characterized by vertical letter stress, uniform stress and absence of serifs. For example, Helvetica, which laces the small extensions on the ascenders and descenders. Related Term: *serif*.

Script (Invitation) Type

One of the five major typeface classifications. One in which the letters are modeled to resemble handwriting; non-joining letters are called cursive script. Scripts come in a variety of weights of formal and informal styles.

Serif

(1) One of three variables in alphabet design; refers to small strokes that are, usually, a perpendicular line found at the end of the unconnected or finishing stroke. Used to provide visual balance to the character shape. Serifs may vary in weight, length and shape, and contribute greatly to the style of the typeface. (2) One of the five classes of type. Related Term: *sans serif*.

Signature

A group of pages that are all printed on the same sheet of paper.

Spot Color

The selective addition of a single solid (or screened) nonprocess color printed using one separation plate, as opposed to a process color printed using two or more separation plates.

Stationery

A collective term applied to letterheads, envelopes, business cards, and other printed materials for correspondence. These types of projects lean toward paper with a high cotton content or "linen" paper.

Symbol

A visual metaphor to use interchangeably with an idea or concept.

Tabloid

A publication format usually about half the size of a broadsheet.

Technical Illustration

A specialized segment of editorial illustration, technical illustration is more prevalent today due to the greater use of computers for graphics and layout. Technical illustration includes schematics, diagrams, charts, and maps; work can be as simple as a line drawing to illustrate product assembly, as complicated as a highly-detailed drawing of an interior combustion mechanism, or anything in between.

Thumbnails

Sketches of different ideas for a design.

Tracking

(1) Often a term used by typographers in place of overall letterspacing. (2) In desktop and digital publishing, a feature in some layout and word processing software packages which reduces the set width of all selected characters by a fixed amount, effectively moving every one of them closer together. Usually not a mathematical value which can be specified, but one of several predefined options such as "none," "tight," "very tight," "loose," "very loose," and "normal." Not to be confused with kerning, which only moves selected characters together for better appearance.

Type Family

A set of fonts that share a common letterform construction. The fonts within a family are closely related, using variations of the basic letterform. A font designer will create a master font, then consistently alter one feature, such as character width or weight, to create another font within the same family. Some common variations are extended, condensed, outline, bold, and thin; regardless of the treatment, the original font is still recognizable.

Varnishing

An over-coating process usually done on press, sometimes even at the same time the piece is being printed. Varnish may be clear or tinted and be dull or gloss in finish. It is simply carried in an ink fountain in place of ink, and applied with a separate image carrier which details the portions of the sheet to be coated. Varnish is applied to printed matter often to enhance halftones, to makes black "blacker" or denser and to increase contrast and overall visual image. Varnish will also protect the printed piece from scuffing and finger marks. Dense blacks and dark color are unusually susceptible to showing the effects of wear and tear, particularly on glossy paper. Varnishing is usually reserved for high-gloss sheets. Rough-surfaced paper generally doesn't benefit from it.

Workflow

The process of queuing, tracking and otherwise managing the production, documents, work items, and collections of documents and work items as they progress from entry into the system and through the various individuals or offices in the organization until a business process is completed.

Index

a

absorbency
  ink 89
abstraction 21, 141
action 142
advertising 127, 133
Aesthetics of Consumerism 133
Aldus 65
amplify 142
analogies 14
AOL 148
art posters 124
art publications 112
artwork
  mechanical 53
Associated Press Stylebook 68
asymmetrical balance 46
attitudes 11
audience
  target 11

b

balance 45
  types of 46
  and page layout 60
Bauhaus 7
binding 85
bit depth 82
black
  symbolism of 29
  ink 60
  and process color printing 80
blue
  symbolism of 28
body copy 65
  and web design 149
bold 65
book
  covers 122
  publishing 122
  paper considerations 90
booklet 86
borders 53
brainstorming 13, 139
  visual 16

brand design 24
brand loyalty 133
branding 127
  and color 78
brightness of paper 89
browsers 145
burn out and creative block 19
business cards 127
business opportunities 125

c

calendars 123
campaign
  developing a 143
canvas 89
captions 53
catalog design 113
categories
  of type 65
cd-rom 151
characteristics of a logo 127
Chicago Manual of Style 68
children's publications 112
cigar-store indian 133
clarity
  picture 93
classified newspaper ad 139
cliché
  dealing with 26
client 128
clothes designer 9
cms 82
cmyk 79
code
  for web pages 145
coherence in page layout 54
collaboration 7
color 77
  memory 78
  paper 88
  viewing conditions 83
color 14
  and web design 147
  and web page design 79
  proofs 34
  symbolism 78

  web safe palette 152
color chart
  process 80
color management 82
color schemes 124
color symbolism 26
columns 56
  and layout 54
commercial printing 85
common page sizes 86
community 141
comparisons
  and informational graphics 118
complacency 8
complimentary colors 79
composition of photographs 94
composition 53, 54
Compuserve 148
condensed type 65
consumer 134
consumerism
  aesthetics of 133
container 43, 54
  and photography 94
content 111
contract
  limited usage 122
copy
  body 65
corporate identity 127
counter display 135
creative block
  dealing with 18
creativity
  definition of 8
  five forces of 7
curiosity 7
cyan 80

d

decorative type 66
demographics 10
design
  multimedia 151
design and illustration 117
  high-traffic 90

1

design and illustration (cont...)
packaging 137
publication 111
designer 9
graphic 13
designing for the web 145
desktop publishing 53
dial-up modem 150
diecutting 92
direct mail 90, 139
direction of a line 62
display
point of purchase 133
display typefaces 66
dividers
shelf 135
download time and web design 150
duotones 81

e

e-machines 145
editorial illustration 120
educational publications 112
effects and photographs 99
email 145
embossing 92
emotional content of a line 64
ethical considerations 119
ethical guidelines
gag 127
exclusive rights 122
Explorer
Internet 148
extended type 65
extenders
shelf 135

f

families
font 65
fee 121
figure/ground relationship 50
file
inspiration 9
file size
and web design 150
filters for photographs 99
fine art 122
fine art media 79
finishing 85
finishing choices 91
five forces of creativity 7
floating object
photographs as a 98
focal point of a page 58
focus
clarity of 93
foil stamping 92
folding 91

font 65
fonts and web design 149
formal
balance 46
formats
standard sizes 53
framing the subject 95
frustration 7
fueling creatively 9

g

gag handbook of pricing and ethical guidelines 127
gamut and color printing 81
genre 122
Gestalt Theory of Visual Organization 62
glossy paper 89
goals 19
graphic designer 9, 13
graphics
information 117
graphics filters 99
gravity-fed displays 135
greeking 55
green
symbolism of 27
grey
symbolism of 29
grids
for layouts 54
Gropius, Walter 7
guides 54

h

hallmarks of good logos 128
Harris, Daniel 133
headline 65
headlines 53
for web pages 147
heraldry and symbolism 23
hierarchy of human needs 24, 141
how to see 7
html 145
hypertext markup language 145
hyphenated words 56

i

icons 25
idea book 9
ideas
stimulating 7
identification 133
identity
corporate 127
illustration 117
editorial 120
technical 119

Illustrators, Society of 125
imagery 8
images 93
imagination 13
impact 133
implication of design 62
imposition 87
impressionist painters 21
impulse buying 133
industrial revolution 7
infographics 117
informal balance 46
information 133
information graphics 117
ink absorbency 89
inkjet printers 35
inspiration 7
file 9
interactive cd-roms 152
interactive kiosks 153
interface for multimedia design 153
interior color schemes 124
Internet 145
Internet Explorer 148
intuition 7
italic 65

j

job boards 125

k

kerning 68
kiosks 135
interactive 153
know your market 10

l

lamination 92
landscapes 22
layout 53
and efficiency 53
development of a 54
makeovers 59
layouts for pictures 97
leading 68
legal 86
letter 86
letter form 65
letter spacing 68
letterhead 91, 127
libel manual 68
limited usage contract 122
line direction 62
line of sight 96
lines
and the design process 61
as objects 61
logos 15, 127

m

magenta 80
makeovers 59
management
color 82
maps 90
margins 54, 56
market
knowing your 10
understanding your 141
master pages 54
matte 89
meaning of colors 77
mechanical
artwork 53
media communications 133
memory colors 78
menus 90
metaphor
visual 22
metaphors 8
mezzotint 99
modem 150
modern symbolism 23
monitors 82
mood and type selection 71
motivation 7
motivational psychology 24
multimedia 146
multimedia design 151

n

nationality 11
negative and positive space 49
Netscape Communicator 148
niche markets 113

o

objects
lines 61
optical properties of paper 89
organization of web sites 146
overwork and creative block 19

p

packaging 90, 136
special concerns for 137
packaging 133
page
common sizes 86
focal point of a 58
proportion 60
page setup 53
pages
master 54
Pantone 35, 80
P.A.P.A. 142

paper 85
optical properties of 89
selecting 90
paper type, color, and texture 88
pastel 84
peer approval 141
pen-and-ink 99
people
pictures of 96
perception 127
color 77
perspective
changing your 10
photography
fashion 22
physical characteristics of lines 61
physical limitation 85
pi (symbol) type 66
pictures
using effective 93
pink
symbolism of 28
pixels 150
pms 81
point-of-purchase (POP) 133
types of 135
positive and negative space 49
postal service
and size considerations 88
postcards and reply cards 90
posters 123
art 124
production considerations for 86
premium display 135
presentation materials 127
presentations 151
primaries 80
printers
inkjet 35
printing 31
commercial 85
printing processes 79
process mapping 35
process color 79
process color chart 80
procrastination and creative block 18
production process 31
projects 101
promise 142
promotional package 138
proofs 31, 34, 142
high-end color 35
types of 34
propaganda 24
proportion and page layout 60
publication design 111

publications
art 112
categories of 111
children's 112
educational 112
technical 112
publishing
book 122
desktop 53
puns 8
purple
symbolism of 28

r

race 11
radial balance 46
radiating lines 64
rationalization 18
readability
improving 59
red
symbolism of 28
regular type 65
relationship
figure/ground 50
of shapes and containers 43
Renaissance art 22
reproduction
reproduction 77
resolution 34
rgb color 82
rhymes 14
rhythm and page layout 58
role models 11
rotating displays 135
roughs 31, 33
rules and borders 60

s

scrapbook 9
script (invitation) type 66
security 141
serif type 65
setup
page 53
sex 141
shape/container relationship 43, 54
examples of 45
shapes
arrangement of 44
shelf extenders 135
shoppers' characteristics 11
sight
line of 96
signature 87
site map 147
sketchbook 10

sketches
  and the production process 33
slogans 140
smoothness of paper 89
society of illustrators 125
source of creativity 8
sourcebook 9
space
  positive and negative 49
  use of 45
space between columns 54
special effects 99
specialty inks 81
spot color 79, 80
standard sizes for page layouts 53
stationary and letterhead 91
strokes and type 65
structured formatting 56
Style
  Chicago Manual of 68
style
  of rules and borders 60
Stylebook
  Associated Press 68
subject
  framing for photograph 95
subliminal messages 44
survival 141
symbol
  type 66
symbolism 22, 141
  color 26, 78
  modern 23
  medieval 23
symbols 22
symmetrical balance 46
synonyms 14

t
tabloid 86
talent 9
target audience 11
technical illustration 119
technical publications 112
technical publishing 111
template
  layout 54
tension 64
texture of paper 88
theory
  color 77
thickness
  line 62
thumbnails 32
  and the production process 31
thumbnails
  and type selection 73
title 65
title bar 60
tracking 68
trademarks 127
tripods 94
Trumatch 80
Twenty Ads that Shook the World 139
Twitchell, James B. 139
type
  decorative 66
  greek 55
  selecting 60
  guidelines for using 69
type categories 65
type families 67
typesetting 111
typography 65

u
unity and layout 58
upc 137
usage 122

v
varnish 92
varnish 81
viewing
  color 83
visual brainstorming 16
visual information 7
visual interest
  creating 56
visual metaphor 22, 141
visual overload 25
visual rhythm
  cosiderations for creating 58

w
web
  browsers 148
  designing for the 145, 150
  safe color palette 82
web safe color palette 152
web tv 82, 145
weight 60
white
  symbolism of 26
words
  brainstorming with 14
work-for-hire 121
workflow
  web 146

y
yellow 80
  symbolism of 27
yellow pages 139

z
z as a layout consideration 57

FLORIDA TECHNICAL COLLEGE LIBRARY
12689 CHALLENGER PARKWAY
SUITE 130
ORLANDO, FL 32826